More Team Games for Trainers

Carolyn Nilson is the author of thirteen other books on training. They are:

Training Program Workbook and Kit (Prentice Hall, 1989)

Training for Non-Trainers (Amacom, 1990)

Training for Non-Trainers (Amacom [paperback], 1991)

Training for Non-Trainers (Juan Granica [Buenos Aires], 1994

How to Manage Training (Amacom, 1991)

How to Start a Training Program in Your Growing Business (Amacom, 1992)

Trainer's Complete Guide to Management & Supervisory Development (Prentice Hall, 1992)

Team Games for Trainers (McGraw-Hill, 1993)

Peer Training (Prentice Hall, 1994)

Games That Drive Change (McGraw-Hill, 1995)

Training & Development Yearbook 1996-97 (Prentice Hall, 1996)

Training & Development Yearbook 1997 (Prentice Hall, 1997)

Training & Development Yearbook 1998 (Prentice Hall, 1998)

How to Manage Training, 2nd edition (Amacom, 1998)

Complete Games Trainers Play II (co-author with Scannell & Newstrom) (Mcgraw-Hill, 1997)

More Team Games for Trainers

Carolyn Nilson

McGraw-Hill

New York   San Francisco   Washington, D.C.   Auckland   Bogotá
Caracas   Lisbon   London   Madrid   Mexico City   Milan
Montreal   New Delhi   San Juan   Singapore
Sydney   Tokyo   Toronto

Library of Congress Cataloging-in-Publication Data

Nilson, Carolyn D.
    More team games for trainers   /   Carolyn Nilson.
       p.   cm.
    Sequel to author's: Team games for trainers. New York : McGraw
-Hill, c1993.
     ISBN 0-07-046590-8 (pbk.)
      1. Teams in the workplace—Problems, exercises, etc.   2. Group
games. 3. Educational games.   I. Nilson, Carolyn D.   Team games
for trainers.   II. Title.
HD66.N548   1997
658. 4'02—dc21   97-41224
                                                  CIP

McGraw-Hill

A Division of The McGraw·Hill Companies

    3 4 5 6 7 8 9 0 MAL/MAL 9 0 2 1 0

ISBN 0-07-046590-8

*The sponsoring editor for this book was Richard Narramore, the editing
supervisor was Fred Dahl, and the production supervisor was Tina
Cameron. It was typeset in Baskerville by Inkwell Publishing Services.*

Printed and bound by Malloy Litho.

McGraw-Hill book are available at special quality discounts to use
as premiums and sales promotions, or for use in corporate
training programs. For more information, please write to the
Director of Special Sales, McGraw-Hill, 11 West 19th Street, New
York, NY 10011. Or contact your local bookstore.

 This book is printed on recycled, acid-free paper
containing a minimum of 50% recycled, de-inked fiber.

To my children:
Kristen, Queen of Creativity, and Eric, King of Magic!

Contents

Introduction   *xv*

Section One. Putting People First

1.   **Baggage**   *3*

2.   **Now and Then**   *5*

3.   **Role Call**   *9*

4.   **Plot Success**   *13*

5.   **Resistance and Reinforcement**   *17*

6.   **What Gets Counted Gets Done**   *21*

7.   **Zoo**   *25*

8.   **Paralysis**   *27*

9.   **Go, Team!**   *31*

10.   **Roving Reporter**   *33*

11.   **The Law of the Hammer**   *35*

12.   **Substitution**   *39*

13.   **Reality Check**   *41*

14.   **Milestones**   *43*

15.   **Diversity Range Finder**   *47*

16.   **What Did You Have to Leave at Home?**   *51*

17.   **Good for Us!**   *53*

18.   **Outstanding!**   *57*

19.   **A Better Phone List**   *59*

20.   **Celebrate Success**   *61*

21.   **Guardian Angel**   *63*

22.   **Free Lunch**   *67*

23.   **More Honest Online**   *69*

24.   **Create a Monster**   *71*

25.   **Chill**   *73*

26.   **What Do You Feel?**   *77*

27.   **Which Mentor?**   *79*

28.   **Bootlegging**   *81*

29.   **Card Deck Problem Identifier**   *83*

30.   **Human Factors Tally**   *91*

Section Two. Team Learning

31.   **Upside Down Training**   *97*

32.   **Mapping How Things Are**   *101*

33.   **Plan-Do-Check-Act for Teams**   *103*

34.   **The Plagues of Hierarchy**   *107*

35.   **Valued Leader**   *109*

36.   **Hat Trick**   *113*

37.   **It's Not How Much You Know…**   *117*

38.   **Recipe For Success**   *119*

39.   **Letter Bomb**   *123*

40.   **Business As <u>Un</u>usual**   *125*

41.   **Inquiry Skills**   *127*

42.   **Going to Grandma's**   *131*

43.   **Smoky Billows**   *133*

44.   **Listen Up**   *135*

45.   **Thinking about Thinking**   *137*

46.   **Not *the* Truth, But *My* Truth**   *139*

47.   **Drafting the "Dialogue Bill of Rights"**   *141*

48.   **Say, What?**   *145*

49.   **Through the Looking Glass**   *147*

50.   **Left-Hand Column**   *149*

51.   **Upside and Downside**   *151*

52.   **White Space**   *153*

53.   **I Own This Business**   *155*

54.   **80/20 and 50/5**   *157*

55.   **Diamonds Are a Team's Best Friend**   *159*

56.   **It's a Numbers Game**   *161*

57.   **360 Degrees Online**   *165*

58.   **Snow Whites and Grumpies**   *169*

59.   **Treasure Hunt**   *171*

60.   **360-Degree Follow-Up**   *175*

61.   **Toy Box**   *177*

62.   **Discovering Digital Literacy**   *179*

63.   **Daily Walk on the Web**   *183*

Section Three. Unleashing Creativity

64.   **Temperature Readout**   *187*

65.   **Peanut Butter Sandwich**   *191*

66.   **Step Right Up**   *193*

67.   **Light and Shadow**   *197*

68.   **Biology 101**   *201*

69.   **Knights of the Round Table**   *203*

70.   **Shop 'Til You Drop**   *205*

71.   **Disconnect the Dots**   *207*

72.   **PTS Syndrome**   *209*

73.   **Job Modeling**   *211*

74.   **Disturbing the Peace**   *213*

75.   **City on a Hill**   *215*

76.   **"I Have a Dream"**   *217*

77.   **Think-*ing***   *219*

78.   **Crystal Ball**   *221*

79.   **Fashion Show**   *223*

80.   **Expert System**   *227*

81.   **Clouds**   *231*

82.   **Play Ball!**   *233*

83.   **A Better Game**   *235*

84.   **Mindmapping**   *237*

85.   **Friendly Robots**   *241*

86.   **Open Up**   *245*

87.   **Castle**   *247*

88.   **Oracle**   *249*

89.   **Vices of the Virtual**   *253*

90.   **Hypertext Hurdles**   *255*

91.   **Tell Me a Different Story**   *259*

92.   **Obstacle Course**   *261*

93.   **Past Is Prologue**   *263*

94.   **If You Were CIO...**   *265*

95.   **Personal Trainer**   *267*

96.   **Triple Self-Portrait**   *269*

97.   **Behind the Scenes**   *273*

98.   **Fishtank**   *275*

99.   **Interior Decorator**   *277*

100.   **Tell Me You Love Me**   *279*

The Game Finder Grid
Find the Training Game for Your Team's Need

SECTION ONE. PUTTING PEOPLE FIRST

Game #	page	needs analysis	improving communication	evaluation	roles and expectations	individualism within teams	problem solving	process improvement	recognition	trust
1. BAGGAGE	3						X			
2. NOW AND THEN	5	X								
3. ROLE CALL	9				X					
4. PLOT SUCCESS	13	X								
5. RESISTANCE AND REINFORCEMENT	17	X				X				
6. WHAT GETS COUNTED GETS DONE	21	X			X			X		
7. ZOO	25				X					
8. PARALYSIS	27	X								
9. GO, TEAM!	31	X			X					
10. ROVING REPORTER	33	X	X							
11. THE LAW OF THE HAMMER	35		X			X				
12. SUBSTITUTION	39				X			X		
13. REALITY CHECK	41		X		X	X				X
14. MILESTONES	43	X	X	X				X		
15. DIVERSITY RANGE FINDER	47		X			X	X	X	X	
16. WHAT DID YOU HAVE TO LEAVE AT HOME?	51		X		X					X
17. GOOD FOR US!	53			X	X			X	X	
18. OUTSTANDING	57					X			X	
19. A BETTER PHONE LIST	59		X			X				
20. CELEBRATE SUCCESS	61		X						X	
21. GUARDIAN ANGEL	63					X	X	X		X
22. FREE LUNCH	67					X				X
23. MORE HONEST ONLINE	69	X	X							
24. CREATE A MONSTER	71				X					X
25. CHILL	73		X					X		
26. WHAT DO YOU FEEL?	77			X		X				
27. WHICH MENTOR?	79	X			X	X				
28. BOOTLEGGING	81				X	X		X		X
29. CARD DECK PROBLEM IDENTIFIER	83	X					X	X		
30. HUMAN FACTORS TALLY	91			X		X	X			

The Game Finder Grid (continued)
Find the Training Game for Your Team's Need
SECTION TWO. TEAM LEARNING

Team Fundamentals

Game #	page	needs analysis	improving communication	evaluation	roles and expectations	individualism within teams	problem solving	process improvement	recognition	trust
31. UPSIDE DOWN TRAINING	97					X				
32. MAPPING HOW THINGS ARE	101	X						X		
33. PLAN-DO-CHECK-ACT FOR TEAMS	103			X				X		
34. THE PLAGUES OF HIERARCHY	107	X		X						X
35. VALUED LEADER	109	X		X	X					
36. HAT TRICK	113									X
37. IT'S NOT HOW MUCH YOU KNOW…	117	X			X					
38. RECIPE FOR SUCCESS	119	X			X					
39. LETTER BOMB	123		X			X	X			
40. BUSINESS AS UNUSUAL	125	X					X			
41. INQUIRY SKILLS	127			X			X	X		
42. GOING TO GRANDMA'S	131							X		
43. SMOKY BILLOWS	133	X				X				
44. LISTEN UP	135		X							
45. THINKING ABOUT THINKING	137		X					X		
46. NOT THE TRUTH, BUT MY TRUTH	139	X	X							
47. DRAFTING THE "DIALOGUE BILL OF RIGHTS"	141		X		X			X		
48. SAY, WHAT?	145		X					X		
49. THROUGH THE LOOKING GLASS	147	X		X		X				
50. LEFT-HAND COLUMN	149	X	X	X						
51. UPSIDE AND DOWNSIDE	151	X			X					
52. WHITE SPACE	153	X					X			
53. I OWN THIS BUSINESS	155			X	X	X				
54. 80/20 AND 50/5	157	X		X				X		
55. DIAMONDS ARE A TEAM'S BEST FRIEND	159	X						X		
56. IT'S A NUMBERS GAME	161			X					X	
57. 360 DEGREES ONLINE	165			X						
58. SNOW WHITES AND GRUMPIES	169			X						
59. TREASURE HUNT	171			X					X	
60. 360-DEGREE FOLLOW-UP	175			X	X	X		X		
61. TOY BOX	177	X				X		X		
62. DISCOVERING DIGITAL LITERACY	179	X						X		
63. DAILY WALK ON THE WEB	183	X				X				

The Game Finder Grid (continued)
Find the Training Game for Your Team's Need
SECTION THREE. UNLEASHING CREATIVITY

Team Fundamentals

Game #	page	needs analysis	improving communication	evaluation	roles and expectations	individualism within teams	problem solving	process improvement	recognition	trust
64. TEMPERATURE READOUT	187	X								
65. PEANUT BUTTER SANDWICH	191	X						X		
66. STEP RIGHT UP	193	X					X			
67. LIGHT AND SHADOW	197			X		X				
68. BIOLOGY 101	201	X						X		
69. KNIGHTS OF THE ROUND TABLE	203	X			X					
70. SHOP 'TIL YOU DROP	205	X						X		
71. DISCONNECT THE DOTS	207	X						X		
72. PTS SYNDROME	209	X	X			X				
73. JOB MODELING	211				X	X				
74. DISTURBING THE PEACE	213		X							
75. CITY ON A HILL	215		X		X					
76. "I HAVE A DREAM"	217		X		X					
77. THINK-ING	219							X		
78. CRYSTAL BALL	221							X		
79. FASHION SHOW	223				X					
80. EXPERT SYSTEM	227				X	X		X		
81. CLOUDS	231	X		X			X			
82. PLAY BALL!	233				X					
83. A BETTER GAME	235	X					X	X		
84. MINDMAPPING	237		X		X	X				
85. FRIENDLY ROBOTS	241				X			X		
86. OPEN UP	245		X				X			
87. CASTLE	247		X		X	X				
88. ORACLE	249	X				X				
89. VICES OF THE VIRTUAL	253	X	X	X						
90. HYPERTEXT HURDLES	255		X	X						
91. TELL ME A DIFFERENT STORY	259	X								
92. OBSTACLE COURSE	261							X		
93. PAST IS PROLOGUE	263					X				
94. IF YOU WERE CIO…	265	X				X				
95. PERSONAL TRAINER	267	X	X	X	X	X		X		

The Game Finder Grid (continued)

Find the Training Game for Your Team's Need

SECTION THREE. UNLEASHING CREATIVITY
(continued)

Team Fundamentals

Game #	page	Needs analysis	improving communication	evaluation	roles and expectations	individualism within teams	problem solving	process improvement	recognition	trust
96. TRIPLE SELF-PORTRAIT	269		X			X				
97. BEHIND THE SCENES	273	X				X				
98. FISHTANK	275				X			X		
99. INTERIOR DECORATOR	277						X			
100. TELL ME YOU LOVE ME	279					X			X	

Introduction

More Team Games for Trainers follows this author's first games book, *Team Games for Trainers,* to address the needs of teams who've been around for a while and of teams who are just forming. *More Team Games for Trainers* reflects a maturation of the team concept and incorporates the experience base of many successful teams over the years. This book, like the earlier book, is built on the notion that people think, learn, and work together better when they are focused easily and happily on the work at hand—and, of course, on the belief that games can help sharpen that focus. This book, unlike the earlier book, incorporates both the ups and downs of nearly a decade of experience with all sorts of workplace teams. The conceptual base of this new book builds upon the successes of teaming's best practices as well as lessons learned from the failures and frustrations of teams. Both books are full of serious content separated into creative, easy-to-grasp chunks of single-focus ideas, overlaid with detailed procedures, presented clearly and succinctly for the team trainer, leader, or facilitator to use or adapt immediately.

Why More Team Games?

Growing pains. That's the best answer. Like children going through adolescence, workplace teams are growing up, and that process of growing is captured in this book. *More Team Games* include exercises, activities, illustrations, metaphors, and fun approaches to knotty problems associated with the *development and growth* of teams. They are all learning tools, each one based on one very strong, single purpose. Each can be adapted to various situations by any trainer or facilitator.

Some of the important themes running throughout this book are:

- that the nature of the process of teaming is as important to success as is the technical competence of the individual;

- that skill-building in old and new forms of communication is an essential, ongoing task of teams, because the team concept is still difficult to implement in American workplaces where, historically, the outstanding individual has been both revered and rewarded;

- that teams have evolved as managers of critical—not just peripheral—business functions such as product quality, customer needs analysis, policy creation, and salary and performance review; and

- that most people want to do good work with high value for their employers and for themselves.

Guidelines For Using Games

Each game in this book has a "game" structure; that is, each is presented in either a fun format, sometimes called a "game shell," or in a typical job aid or familiar simulation format. Each is meant to stretch the team member's mental approach to the topic or issue and to enable a change in perspective. Games are sometimes said to have "ulterior motives." Problems are presented in new ways through games.

There are few rules for using team games, but there are some general guidelines that can start you off on the right track as a facilitator or trainer. These are:

1. A game is not training; it is the device that focuses the attention of the learner on that which is to be learned.

2. Choose a game carefully to be certain that it supports the points you will make during the training that follows. Don't waste time in pointless play.

3. Be sure that the game you choose fits the time and the size of the group that you will be working with. Practice the "business" of the game ahead privately if you're not sure; time key elements of the "play" in advance, keeping in mind the probable interactions between the people you know you'll have in your training session or team meeting.

4. Check out each game for potential trouble spots, keeping in mind the specific people in your team. Know which elements of the game are likely to trigger showoffs, misunderstanding, or complaints from your particular trainees. Plan ahead to use such moments as opportunities to lead learners into new awareness. Be prepared ahead of time to meet criticism head-on in the name of learning, not defensiveness.

5. Team games are generally group activities. Within this context, however, you, the trainer, must focus on the individuals who are engaged in the

game, which sometimes gets pretty tricky given the pace that games can whip up. Think of game players as learners—individuals who have different rates of endurance, different readiness states, different ways of learning, different emotional needs, different abilities, different risk-taking styles, and a host of other individual differences. Build some flexibility into the procedures and discussion questions of each game to account for the diversity your team demonstrates.

6. Facilitating a team game is a little like doing a magic trick. You as the leader need to keep a kind of parallel processing going: Most games have a "gimmick" or an ulterior motive, a hidden agenda in the name of learning, which the obvious process of play often "covers" or masks. All of this requires the facilitator to train in a kind of parallel processing mode so that the learner arrives at that "a ha!" moment with a truly heightened capacity for learning. Game playing is fun.

7. Games can soften the rough edges of difficult and unfamiliar ways of working together. Team development and growth involve trial and error, pain and passion. Games can help create an environment for shared values, deeper communication, collegiality, and emotional openness. They can provide the setting for mental stretch, exercising both left-brain and right-brain abilities. Team games are meant to engage and involve learners in new approaches to work. Be prepared to defend the softer side of training when you choose a team game.

What This Book Contains

More Team Games for Trainers is organized into three major sections, each of which contains between 30 and 37 games, for a total of 100 games. The three sections feature issues and topics of concern to developing teams that are growing in depth and breadth of responsibility. In addition, the games in this book intentionally address the fundamentals of learning to work successfully in teams. Within each section, there are games that develop the tools for needs analysis, improving communication, evaluation, fulfilling roles and expectations, facilitating individual growth within the team context, problem solving, process improvement, recognition, and building trust. These areas of team fundamentals are listed at the beginning of each section, with the corresponding games for that section. A cross-referenced matrix including all 100 games appears after the table of contents.

The book's three major sections and some of the content areas within them are:

Putting People First, including harnessing change, before and beyond the bottom line, adding personal value, motivation, expectations, rewards, polishing your stars, dialogue, communication, trust, integrity, discipline, commitment;

Team Learning, including seeking information, turning learning into doing, measuring performance, learning online, coaching, personal trainers, new ways to learn, designing team learning, partnering, process improvement, problem solving, system analysis, decision making, the power of reflection, the functions of language;

Unleashing Creativity, including making diversity work, innovation versus groupthink, the whole in the parts, friendly failures, emotional health, principle-centered work, vision, constraints and limitations, individual self-assessment, baseline and stretch, personality type, quality, technology supports, symbols, ceremony, analogies, and metaphors.

SECTION ONE
Putting People First

Games Listed by Team Training Topic

Game   *Page*

Needs Analysis

2. Now and Then *5*
4. Plot Success *13*
5. Resistance and Reinforcement . . . *17*
6. What Gets Counted Gets Done . . *21*
8. Paralysis *27*
9. Go, Team! *31*
10. Roving Reporter *33*
14. Milestones *43*
23. More Honest Online *69*
27. Which Mentor? *79*
29. Card Deck Problem Identifier . . . *83*

Improving Communication

10. Roving Reporter *33*
11. The Law of the Hammer *35*
13. Reality Check *41*
14. Milestones *43*
15. Diversity Range Finder *47*
16. What Did You Have to Leave
    at Home? *51*
19. A Better Phone List *59*
20. Celebrate Success *61*
23. More Honest Online *69*
25. Chill *73*

Evaluation

14. Milestones *43*
17. Good for Us! *53*
26. What Do You Feel? *77*
30. Human Factors Tally *91*

Roles and Expectations

3. Role Call *9*
6. What Gets Counted Gets Done . . *21*
7. Zoo *25*
9. Go, Team! *31*
12. Substitution *39*
13. Reality Check *41*
16. What Did You Have to Leave
    at Home? *51*
24. Create a Monster *71*
27. Which Mentor? *79*
28. Bootlegging *81*

Individualism within Teams

11. The Law of the Hammer *35*
13. Reality Check *41*
15. Diversity Range Finder *47*
17. Good for Us! *53*
18. Outstanding! *57*
19. A Better Phone List *59*
21. Guardian Angel *63*
22. Free Lunch *67*
26. What Do You Feel? *77*
27. Which Mentor? *79*
28. Bootlegging *81*
30. Human Factors Tally *91*

Problem Solving

1. Baggage *3*
5. Resistance and Reinforcement *17*
15. Diversity Range Finder *47*
21. Guardian Angel *63*
29. Card Deck Problem Identifier *83*
30. Human Factors Tally *91*

Process Improvement

6. What Gets Counted Gets Done *21*
12. Substitution *39*
14. Milestones *43*
15. Diversity Range Finder *47*
17. Good for Us! *53*
21. Guardian Angel *63*
24. Create a Monster *71*
27. Which Mentor? *79*
28. Bootlegging *81*

Recognition

15. Diversity Range Finder *47*
17. Good for Us! *53*
18. Outstanding! *57*
20. Celebrate Success *61*

Trust

13. Reality Check *41*
16. What Did You Have to Leave at Home? *51*
21. Guardian Angel *63*
22. Free Lunch *67*
24. Create a Monster *71*
28. Bootlegging *81*

1

Baggage

Objective

To focus team members' attention on the ways in which things are changing.

Procedure

Place an old beat-up suitcase, opened, in the middle of the floor. Ask team members to sit in a circle around the suitcase.

Give each team member a stack of 8½×11-inch paper—at least 6 sheets per person. A variety of colors will add interest to the game. Have extra paper available at a convenient location near all players.

Instruct team members to write down all of the items of organizational baggage they can think of that they'd like to discard as the team grows and develops. Allow only 1 item per piece of paper. Encourage fast thinking.

As each person finishes writing down an item of baggage, he or she crumples the paper and tosses it into the old suitcase. Encourage people to write, crumple, and toss as fast as they can, all together. Get some energy going!

Expect items such as: management sign-offs, time clocks, copy machine logs, limits on library time, fixed lunch hours, etc. If team members are having a hard time getting started, suggest some of these as examples, or simply tell them to write down what bugs them or what they'd like to send off to the next planet.

Set a timer for 20 minutes and give the start command. When the timer goes off, make a big deal about closing up the suitcase, picking it up, and carrying it out the door.

Bring it back in for analysis of contents. Uncrumple each paper, and with the help of an assistant, record the types of baggage on a flip chart or whiteboard. Re-crumple each page after its contents have been recorded, and throw it into a trash can. Ask for a show of hands to indicate how many agree with each item. If your team is 10 or more persons, do a frequency count of responses. A simple show of hands is probably sufficient in a smaller team.

Discussion Questions

Focus discussion on what are no longer valid assumptions about work and work processes at this company, and why these are no longer needed here, as teams have become more advanced, more solid, and more responsible. Keep discussion flowing as long as it is productive.

Use this game as a way both to get problems out into the open and to let team members—all team members—expend some emotion safely about some things that are bothering them. Use it either as a means to discover and define problems, that is, as a problem-definition exercise, or as an introductory piece of the strategic planning necessary for establishing a change agenda. This is a good energizer game to use in a workshop right after lunch, at the end of the day, or as part of a team meeting that could use a little spark of excitement.

Materials

6–10 pieces of blank 8½×11-inch paper, preferably colored, for each team member; a pencil or marker for each team member; an old beat-up suitcase; a flip chart or whiteboard; a trash can.

Approximate Time Required

20 minutes plus discussion time as needed.

2
Now and Then

Objective

To get the team's ideas for their "responsibility agenda" following a manager's or executive's indication of commitment to greater team responsibility for important business functions.

Procedure

Use the overhead transparency master on page 7 with an overhead projector and screen or as a master to copy onto a whiteboard or flip chart. Be sure that all team members can see the chart clearly.

Direct their attention to the four categories across the top of the chart, paying particular attention to the split in the "later" category into 6 months and 12 months.

Read the company's mission statement or other executive memos regarding teams; facilitate a discussion of specific items of responsibility that are in transition. List responsibilities down the left side of the chart. Try to elicit about 30 items.

Team members will then vote by a show of hands as you and they together decide on a rough timeline "now and then" for taking over what were previously management responsibilities. To give team members a chance at leadership, ask various team members to facilitate the discussion of 5 items each until all 30 items are completed with a check mark in one of the four columns, representing a consensus of the team on each item.

Save the last 10 items for team members with the most experience and skill at facilitation. Be careful that energy doesn't dissipate near the end of the exercise. Save your best for last.

Discussion Questions

Take your cues from the mission statement and the words your executive(s) have said. Take them seriously and encourage team members to put themselves in the position of managers as

Notes

they separate out the various kinds of things managers do—the different kinds of responsibilities—that hereafter will be done by teams.

Some typical responsibilities that managers divest to teams are: schedule vacations, plan overtime, handle discipline, monitor and ensure safety, make work assignments, train new employees, coordinate flow of work, establish performance standards, evaluate performance. If team members are having trouble, suggest that they think in terms of major categories such as benefits, problems, safety, EEO issues, job design, pay, and performance.

By going through a matrix exercise like this, team members are encouraged to analyze and to think in discrete items rather than in holistic terms. Analysis exercises are necessary as a first step in creating plans. This is a typical left-brain exercise.

Materials

Format "Now and Then," page 7, to use as an overhead transparency master or as a guide for a whiteboard or flip chart; overhead projector and screen.

Approximate Time Required

15–25 minutes.

Now and Then

| RESPONSIBILITIES | NOW | LATER | | NEVER |
		IN 6 MONTHS	IN 12 MONTHS	
1				
2				
3				
4				
5				
6				
7				
8				
9				
10				
11				
12				
13				
14				
15				
16				
17				
18				
19				
20				
21				
22				
23				
24				
25				
26				
27				
28				
29				
30				

3
Role Call

Objective

*To provide a means for team members to
self-select roles within the team, so that all
team members can see each other's
choices.*

Procedure

Ask someone to volunteer to be a
recorder. This person will keep a tally
of which person(s) choose which roles.
Recording can be done either with pencil and paper at a desk or on a flip
chart or whiteboard for all to see.

Have team members line up as if for
roll call, army-style. Prepare an overhead transparency (handwritten is fine,
as in the sample found on page 11) listing all of the possible roles a team
member can play in addition to the behaviors inherent in his or her job performance. Show the transparency as the
team is lining up. Pace in front of them
like a drill sergeant, barking "Heads up,
shoulders back!" Get the point across
that each one at this very moment must
stand up and be counted.

Instruct the team members to look at
the overhead and think about what one
role each would like to play during the
next month (or some other specific
time) as this new project is initiated.
Give them 30 seconds or so to read the
overhead.

Then begin the role call. Starting at the
head of the line, call each person by
first name and say, "Bob, your role,
sir?" or "Kristen, your role, ma'am?"
and wait for the response. It's okay if
more than one person wants the same
role. Negotiate the differences later. For
now, just record who wants what role.
Continue through the line systematically until all team members have identified their roles. Allow an "other" response if someone has a legitimate role
that you've forgotten to put on the overhead, but be sure that this other role is
named.

After the role definition, tell the team
to be "at ease" and return to their seats.
Facilitate a negotiation session to bal-

Notes

ance the roles, so that each person comes away with a role that he or she can live with and in which learning and growth can occur.

Discussion Questions

These are some of the more common roles performed by team members. Add your own to complete the field of choices.

Researcher	Problem solver
Standards setter	Coordinator
Devil's advocate	Documenter
Experimenter	Monitor
Troubleshooter	Strategist
Traffic cop	Planner
Cheerleader	Ethicist/team conscience
Clown/tension reliever	Networker
Salesperson	Feedback giver
Crap detector	Negotiator
Meeting convener	Listener

If team members don't choose a role or roles that you believe are critical to the success of the team project, focus on these and find out why no one chose them.

> It is important, especially at the start of a new project or at the beginning of a new team performance measurement period, that team members understand that process is as important as job skill in successful teamwork. It is also important that each team member be expected to fulfill a role, or roles, during the team's project. This game builds that expectation.

Materials

An overhead transparency similar to the one on page 11; flip chart and marker or other recording materials.

Approximate Time Required

20–30 minutes.

Role Call

strategist

Cheerleader

coordinator

problem solver

experimenter

Conscience*

Devil's advocate

salesperson

documenter

monitor

4

Plot Success

Objective

To analyze a team's present composition regarding the two dimensions of management and leadership. To analyze the team's composition at a mid-project assessment point.

Procedure

This is an exercise to be done individually by team members during a team meeting. Make copies of the matrix on page 15 and distribute one to each team member. This will be used to make a scatter plot graph.

Each team member is represented by an *X* on the matrix, but is unnamed. The point is to see the gathering of *X*s, or plot marks, that indicate the weight of the team in one direction or another. The four quadrants of the matrix represent strong and weak, leadership and management. A finished scatter plot might look something like this:

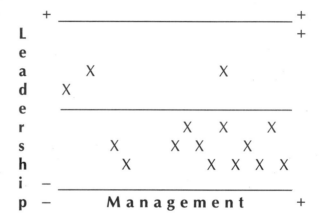

This scatter plot represents a team of 15 persons, each of whom is represented by an *X* on the matrix. This *X* is the team member's judgment about where team members fit on a scale rating strong to weak leaders and managers. In this example, the team is judged by one team member as being too full of managers. Managers at the expense of leaders will be planners and not visionaries, controllers and not facilitators who empower others. Teams that are out of balance this way will not succeed. Show the team members how to do a scatter plot, using this or a similar scatter plot as a sample.

Notes

Instruct team members to consider each member of the team individually, systematically scanning the assembled team in silence so that no one is omitted. Instruct each team member to place an *X* on the matrix in the place that best describes his or her best judgment about where each individual belongs on the matrix, according to his or her behavior on the team thus far.

After all have completed their separate plots, facilitate a discussion about how and why team members voted the way they did. Ask the team to figure out how to make adjustments to either the managerial or leadership behaviors of the team so that the success of the project can be assured as they go forward from this in-process assessment.

Discussion Questions

Be sure that the discussion does not degenerate into a put-down of either managers or leaders. Both are necessary for team success, but often, teams do not take the time to carefully assess how the team is actually doing in each of these dimensions. Managers tend to keep processes going forward, while leaders drive changes. Try to encourage a discussion of team-appropriate management behaviors; look for new characteristics of management such as facilitating, designing, negotiating, and providing support, not just the same old directing, controlling, and disciplining.

> Two excellent current books contain good discussions about leadership problems and the issues involved in balancing management with leadership. These are: *Why Teams Don't Work* by Harvey Robbins and Michael Finley, Princeton, NJ: Peterson's/Pacesetter Books, 1995, pp. 80ff; and *Leading Change* by John P. Kotter, Cambridge, MA: Harvard Business School Press, 1996, chapter 4, "Creating the Guiding Coalition."

Materials

A scatter plot matrix, as on page 15, for each team member.

Approximate Time Required

30–45 minutes, depending on the size of the team.

Plot Success

L E A D E R S H I P

M A N A G E M E N T

5

Resistance and Reinforcement

Objective

To engage team members in doing a classic force-field analysis of what is and what could be, using any current team situation as the focus. Examples include: relationships within the team; the team's external relationships with other teams in the company; the team's customer relations; the team's contribution to profit or sales; etc.

Procedure and Discussion

Do this at a team meeting to give team members experience with using a tried and true tool for organizational diagnosis.

Explain force-field analysis as an analysis of forces. It is a diagnostic technique most readily used to define a problem and suggest a clear path toward resolution of that problem. It is often the critical first step in separating problem definition from problem solving. Too often teams, in their exuberance, try to solve problems before they define what the problems actually are.

Use the example of relationships within the team to illustrate the technique. Have each team member work separately. Present an overview of force-field analysis using the following diagram, specifying the ideal situation at the top of the page, the worst possible situation at the bottom of the page, and the current situation in between these.

ideal situation:

current situation: _____

worst possible situation:

During the exercise, each team member will have to define what he or she believes to be the ideal, the worst possible, and the current situations. These will form the foundation of the discussion that follows. As you begin to work, ask the team to focus on the current situation. Suggest that they fill in the blank: "The current situation regarding relationships within this team is: _____."

Then fill in the ideal situation definition; then do the worst possible situa-

Notes

tion. After the three definitions have been completed individually, facilitate a discussion of the current situation, asking team members how they defined it, and reaching a consensus on what the true definition is. Record this on a flip chart or whiteboard for all to see.

Before going on to get consensus on the other two situations, introduce the idea of competing forces, that is, the forces that are counterbalanced on the current situation. Using this diagram can help:

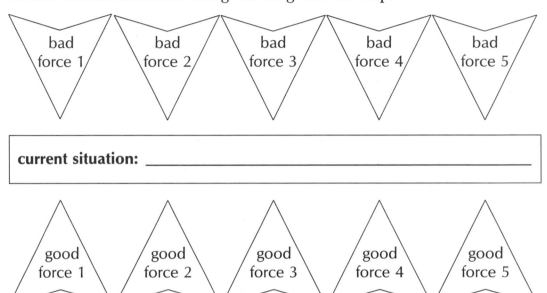

Explain that there are both altruistic and bottom line forces pushing up from the bottom to move the current situation up toward the ideal situation, reinforcing forces out of one's beliefs and value systems as well as good, solid business forces that encourage change. At this point, ask team members to focus on the bottom set of good forces pushing up toward the ideal. These forces can help a team make adjustments to the current situation.

On the other hand, the top set of forces bearing down on the current situation are bad forces, those that resist change and restrain progress toward the ideal. Alas, too often, restraining forces are stronger than reinforcing forces and work to maintain a problematic status quo. Give the team a few minutes to define their own individual driving forces (good forces) and restraining forces (bad forces). Suggest that each team member try to define five of each kind of force, resulting in a set of good forces and a set of bad forces.

If team members are having trouble thinking specifically, here are some ideas you can suggest. Team effectiveness depends on:

- talent and job competence of each person,

- having a clear direction for work of the team,

- systems in place that work well to support the team,
- team work that matters—that is, work that is important and nontrivial,
- efficient procedures,
- rewards for outstanding work,
- appropriate responsibilities,
- opportunities for constructive relationships outside of the team,
- etc.

Now ask team members to define the ideal situation and the worst possible situation. To save time, this can be done orally as a freewheeling discussion. Record the consensus definition on the flip chart or whiteboard.

At this point, open discussion of the sets of forces, dealing with the bad forces (top set) first. Get consensus and record. Then define the good forces (bottom set) and record the consensus. This marks the completion of the basic force-field analysis.

To take the technique a step or two further, ask members to weight all of the forces (bad and good) on a scale of 1 to 5 or 1 to 10. Then group any that seem related and reweight the group. Use what you learned to set plans in motion to work more effectively toward your stated ideal situation, to increase the weight of some of the good forces and decrease the weight of some of the bad forces.

Force-field analysis originally comes from the physical sciences where forces of stress in materials are analyzed and subsequently counterbalanced. Kurt Lewin is generally credited with adapting the model to situations in psychology and social relationships as an organizational diagnosis tool. Force-field analysis is a good way to look at a current situation, often a problem situation, to discover the counterbalancing forces or sets of forces that work against each other to keep things the way they are. Deeper analysis moves the team into stages of problem solving after the initial problem definition is made possible through the tool of force-field analysis.

Trainers are familiar with the traditional needs assessment model of measuring the gap between "what is" and "what should be"; force-field analysis is a tool for thinking about "what is" and "what *could* be." Don't confuse the two models.

Notes

Materials

Pencils and paper for each team member; flip chart or whiteboard and markers for recording the consensus force-field analysis diagram.

Approximate Time Required

15–45 minutes.

6

What Gets Counted Gets Done

Objective

To identify operational improvements–hard results–in the context of the softer side of organizational relationships. To build expectations that the soft organizational goals can be a by-product of the hard results.

Procedure

Use this as an exercise during a team meeting as a way of introducing the subject of setting realistic but "stretch" goals. Follow this introduction with operational goal setting and action planning.

Distribute a "What Gets Counted Gets Done" chart to each team member (see page 23). Read down the left column of types of operational improvement, or have team members read down the column in turn. Ask for suggestions of any more items that should be added to the list. Focus the team's attention on the implicit numbers associated with these items—dollars, percentages, weeks and months, cycle times, numbers of complaints, numbers of items returned, higher yields, number of out of range items, standard deviations, fewer absences, fewer grievances, etc.

Then read across the categories of soft organizational goals: trust, morale, loyalty, commitment, joy, service, support, communication, etc. Ask for suggestions to add to these.

When the lists are complete, ask team members to write the added items on their sheets. Then ask them to place a check mark in any column of the soft goals that will be affected by the hard results item. Continue through the chart row by row. Use this exercise as a sensitizing exercise to alert team members to look for soft spinoffs from rigorous processes of counting. This is not a plan; it is a sensitivity exercise to be used before planning begins.

Discussion Questions

Focus on how people feel about relating goals for the business to the more altruistic goals of organizational health.

Notes

Suggest that what gets counted gets done, and that organizational change must focus first on the numbers of things that can be counted, measured, evaluated, and changed. Prepare the team to exercise its emotional intelligence to look for positive spinoffs in the areas across the top of the chart. Encourage them to think divergently over and into the organization at the same time they are thinking convergently to set and meet numerical targets.

It's tempting to start this exercise the other way around, that is, with a focus on improving trust, commitment, loyalty, etc. This generally is a mistake because these items are hard to measure and frequently mean different things to different people. Numbers, on the other hand, are unambiguous, definitive, and easy to measure. Most observers feel that if the team sets realistic and stretch numerical goals, and works honestly to achieve them, the other, soft side of organizational life will improve as a consequence.

Materials

A handout of the What Gets Counted Gets Done chart (page 23) for each team member.

Approximate Time Required

20 minutes.

What Gets Counted Gets Done

	trust	morale	loyalty	commitment	joy	communication	support	service
1. More sales								
2. Better margins								
3. Quicker delivery								
4. Higher yields								
5. Shorter development cycles								
6. Lower cost								
7. Fewer complaints								
8. Fewer returns								
9. More inventory turns								
10. Fewer quality defects								
11.								
12.								
13.								
14.								
15.								
16.								
17.								
18.								
19.								
20.								

7
Zoo

Objective

To analyze team dysfunction using the metaphor of zoo animals and techniques of imaging: what "we" think of ourselves and what we think "they" think of us.

Procedure

Separate the team into subgroups of 3 or 4 persons. Send each small group into a breakout room with a flip chart and markers and the following task:

Think of all of the animals in the zoo and the characteristics that make each kind unique—funny, scary, majestic, sinister, raucous, devious, friendly, clever—as well as the physical features that distinguish one kind from another. During this game team members will be asked to assign animal characteristics or attributes to the team. Each breakout room has the task of drawing two zoo animals made up of characteristics and features that exaggerate or symbolize the features of team: one animal to represent what we, the team, think of ourselves; and one animal to represent what others in the company think of the team. The drawing should be a group project, with each person drawing some part of the composite animals. Label the drawings "what we think" and "what they think."

After the drawings are completed, the subgroups return with them to the larger meeting room to post the drawings on the wall and to share them with the full team.

During the discussion, look for discrepancies in perception and talk about them. Lay out the reasons for the discrepancies and begin to plan for correction of whatever dysfunction results from the discrepancies.

Discussion Questions

When the full team is reassembled, facilitate a discussion about untested assumptions, office myths, biases, misperceptions, imbalances, feedback, and gatekeepers. Compare and contrast all

Notes

of the animals to determine similarities and differences. Find out why each small group drew the pictures they did. Encourage the team as a whole to imagine what needs to be done in order to correct problems that are apparent from the symbolic and metaphorical representations.

This game is a variant of the generic imaging/feedback exercise. It is more right-brained than most such exercises which tend to feature written phrases and folded paper successively revealing each side's description, "we" and "they." A third dimension is often added at larger workshops attended by numerous teams: not only what we think they think of us, but what "they" actually think.

This particular game is fun at a workshop or as an energizer any time—it's active and gets everyone involved in drawing what ends up as a cartoon caricature of the team.

Expect outrageous creatures—giraffes' necks with weasels as ears and pumas' bodies with eagles' wings. Who knows, by the time you all finish this one, the team might just have created a mascot!

Materials

Flip chart and markers for the large meeting room and for each breakout room.

Approximate Time Required

30–45 minutes.

8
Paralysis

Objective

To analyze the symptoms, causes, and issues that paralyze the team.

Procedure

Give each team member about 10 self-stick notes, 2×3-inch size. On a whiteboard or a flip chart sheet held horizontally, draw a big empty arrow into which team members will eventually place their self-stick notes. Fill up a standard flip chart page with the arrow. The drawing on page 30 illustrates how the arrow might look. Post this on a wall for all to see.

On each self-stick note, instruct team members to draw a mini-arrow, similar to the one on the wall, with room in it to write a team characteristic. Put the arrow head over the sticky end, like this:

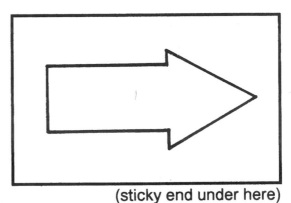

(sticky end under here)

The idea of this game is to define the causes of team paralysis, particularly in the areas of communication, discipline, and other human resource considerations.

Instruct each team member to write one word or short phrase in each arrow on the pack of self-stick notes. After this is done, each team member comes up to the big arrow on the wall and places the small arrows inside of it. The arrow heads of the small arrows can point in exactly the same direction as the big arrow, or can point at any angle that seems appropriate ac-

Notes

cording to the team member's experience of the way things are. Pointing backward is also acceptable.

These are some of the words that could be written on the small arrows. Suggest them to the team before they start writing: pride in work, personal accountability, competence, trust, collegiality, humility, sharing, fairness, energy, efficiency, customer focus, etc. Any team characteristic or goal can be written on the small arrows.

After all small arrows are placed within the big arrow, facilitate a discussion about how to get the smaller arrows in alignment with the big arrow. Encourage team members to move their self-stick note arrows any way they want as they refine their opinions about how things really are.

Discussion Questions

There's a lot written about the notion of alignment, that is, the lining up of personal goals and capacities with the stated organizational or team goals. This game borrows some theory from developmental psychology in which the individual grows and develops within a family that is growing and developing. That is, both entities are moving and changing, hopefully in alignment. This game illustrates the idea that empowerment and participation without direction lead to paralysis. The larger entity is so full of smaller entities pulling and pushing in various uncoordinated and misaligned directions that it cannot go forward.

If, on the other hand, the smaller entities are in alignment and moving in the same direction, the speed and power of movement of the whole are greatly enhanced. This is the concept of "both ... and," not "either ... or." Facilitate a general discussion of some "both ... and" possibilities. Some might be:

teamwork and personal initiative,

discipline and entrepreneurship,

quality assurance and risk taking,

achievement of excellence and setting stretch targets,

decisive leadership and empowered employees.

> This game is an analysis technique for at least identifying some of the places that are out of alignment as the team is trying to move forward. Focus this exercise on identification, leaving the planning for correction until later.

Materials

Pads of 2×3-inch self-stick notes; flip chart paper; markers.

Approximate Time Required

20–40 minutes.

Paralysis

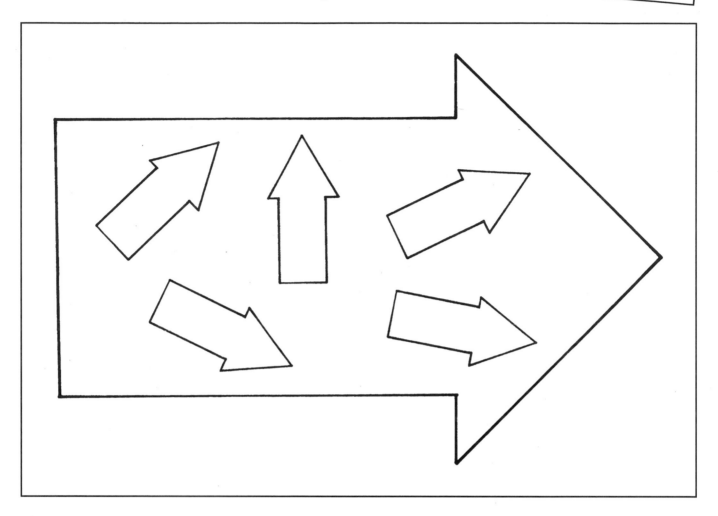

9
Go, Team!

Objective

To sensitize team members to various kinds of teams. To define team roles and relationships within the team itself.

Procedure

At a team meeting, especially the kind of meeting held to take stock of how you're doing as a team, facilitate a freewheeling discussion of a variety of kinds of teams. Do this by leading off with a suggestion that participants focus on relationships within the team.

Ask team members what kind of team they think they are, and how they model the behaviors or roles of sports or performance teams. Continue the exercise as long as it is useful. Adopt a model for your own team behavior that is clear to everyone and go forward. Repeat this exercise monthly or whenever you feel the need to do an in-process assessment of intra-team relationships.

Discussion Questions

When teams form, they often have a fuzzy idea of how they should be working together. This, of course, is because each member has a different experience base of being on a team or supporting a team, and each person makes certain assumptions about what teamwork means.

As teams continue over time, sometimes these differences draw the team apart rather than together, and it's a good idea to pause periodically and re-assess just exactly what kind of team this really is. Here are some possibilities, each of which has a different internal set of rules governing the behavior and relationships of the members of that particular kind of team:

Notes

basketball team	oxen team
swim team	research and development team
soccer team	orchestra
baseball team	madrigal group
football team	Corgi breeder's team
gymnastics team	synchronized swim team
track team	dance team
hockey team	food service team
Little League team	Park & Rec girls' basketball team

Ask team members which kind of team seems most like theirs; or what characteristics of team relationships seem most like relationships within any of the model teams. Ask them to focus on the nature of the team process, as they analyze their own evolving model of teamwork. Send them back to work with a clearer idea of how their own team should be functioning in terms of person-to-person relationships within the team.

In the zeal to tackle new work and important responsibilities, team members often neglect to clarify just what kind of team they are. Everyone knows that team success depends on good relationships among the team members, but often people don't really know what the standards are for those relationships or what the team models are upon which their particular team was fashioned. It helps to take an objective look at these issues periodically as a team matures, because work changes and relationships deepen.

It has been said of an orchestra that music flows through each individual member, not from them. Team members need to know how to be effective conduits; it's the music, after all, that we pay the money to hear.

Materials

None.

Approximate Time Required

10–20 minutes.

10
Roving Reporter

Objective

To interview a random sample of senior managers for answers to the question, "How will the future of this industry be different?" To compare and contrast the answers in order to discern the company's "strategic architecture."

Procedure

Get a list of your company's senior managers and randomly select a group of them to interview. Each interview will be done by a different team member. Select enough managers so that each team member has one manager to interview. Go down the list of managers so that a reasonable sample can be drawn from a wide enough range.

Set a time period, for example three days, in which all interviews should be completed. Set the date with each manager well ahead of time. Have each team member ask the same question:

"How will the future of this industry be different?"

Provide the following instructions to team members:

The question is purposely vague so that the words "future," "industry," and "different" can be defined in many different ways. The object of the interview is to record the managers' answers in whatever form they are given, without the interviewers' defining terms. Use a tape recorder if you expect a long-winded session; otherwise, record notes on paper as the person is speaking and take a few minutes directly after the interview to be sure your notes make sense.

Have team members bring their notes to a team meeting on a predetermined date for discussion. Ask them not to discuss them outside of this meeting.

Discussion Questions

The essential information you are trying to get from the managers is what

Notes

Hamel and Prahalad call a company's "strategic architecture." Managers generally view themselves as designers, architects, and builders of organizations. Their answers to the interview question should provide the team with many ideas about the company's structure and the future vision for it. Mission statements are often generated to fill in the gap between where the company is to date and this strategic vision of how the company will look in some imagined future. This game is an exercise in structure-seeking, however, and not an exercise in visioning or making mission statements.

> Refer to *Competing for the Future* by Gary Hamel and C.K. Prahalad, Boston: Harvard Business School Press, 1994, chapter 5, "Crafting Strategic Architecture." Case studies of the Japanese company, NEC, and the American company, EDS, in this chapter provide examples of companies with clear values and actions regarding development of strategic architecture. Excerpts from chapter 5 could be reprinted for team members to use as preparation for the interviews and as a theoretical foundation for discussion during the team meeting following the interviews.

Materials

An interview form for each team member; reprints (referred to above) for each team member.

Approximate Time Required

20–60 minutes for each interview; 20 minutes for the team discussion.

11
The Law of the Hammer

Objective

To sensitize team members to their own mental models, encouraging them to continuously define and refine their personal mental models.

Procedure

Distribute copies of the poster found on page 37 to each team member at a team meeting at which discussion occurs regarding mental models. Suggest that each team member post The Law of the Hammer in a prominent place to act as a reminder to uncover and deal with one's own mental models. The Law of the Hammer is:

> **"If my only tool is a hammer, everything becomes a nail."**

Spend some time at a team meeting illustrating how mental models work. Use any of the books referenced below, or relate stories from your own experience.

For example, I know that one of my own primary mental models is that of a musician: I often think of projects as compositions, as songs to be sung, operas to be experienced. My vocabulary is full of words such as listen, hear, rhythm, cadence, sing, resonate, vibrate, timbre, drama, stage business, etc. I think about work as one who performs to standards of my own "instrument" in order to make the whole of the music more beautiful in collaboration with other performers. I see lines and phrases as well as chords, both horizontal and vertical at the same time. I know that my interactions with others are affected by my horizontal/vertical mental model: I know that I often get impatient with persons who don't or can't think in both directions at once. My mental models enrich my life, but they also get in my way. I have a friend who is a dancer, and who sees life as a choreographed movement through time and space; I also have a friend who sees life as a series of contests, always with winners and losers. These mental models affect how we talk, write, make decisions, define problems, and solve problems.

Notes

After stimulating the team with some stories like those in the previous paragraph, ask brainstorming-type questions to see if the team can surface any of its members' mental models. That is, facilitate a freewheeling discussion of mental models, with or without handout reprints from the referenced books. Ask team members to define some of their own mental models; ask team members to tell each other what their perceptions are of each other's mental models. Cut off discussion before everyone feels confident about their definitions; the point of this exercise is to stir up interest in mental models, and to send them away from the meeting with more questions than answers and a curiosity to keep the process of self-discovery going.

Revisit the issue at later meetings. Save the matching of team members' own mental models with corporate or team vision statements for another time.

Discussion Questions

As team members begin discussion of their own mental models, they might have trouble thinking so introspectively. Give them some help by asking, "What kinds of words show up in your writing or speaking that could give you clues?" "What kinds of metaphors do you often use?" "Are there certain stereotypes you favor?" "Certain catchphrases you like to use?" "Are you prone to putting 'spin' on what you say or write?" "Do your stories tend to have similar themes, characters, or language?"

Three good books offer excellent background for exploration of mental models. Get copies of these and make them available in your team lending library. If you like to encourage your team to read the works of current business thinkers, you might prepare a handout of excerpts from these books and distribute it to team members at this meeting or as a follow-up to this meeting. The books are: *The Art of Framing* by Gail T. Fairhurst and Robert A. Sarr, San Francisco: Jossey-Bass, 1996, viz., chapters 3, 4, 5, 6; *Frames of Mind* by Howard Gardner, New York: Basic Books, 1985; and *The Fifth Discipline* by Peter Senge, New York: Doubleday Currency, 1990.

Materials

The Law of the Hammer poster for each team member (page 37); (optional) a handout for each team member of excerpts from the three books referenced above.

Approximate Time Required

15–30 minutes.

The Law of the Hammer

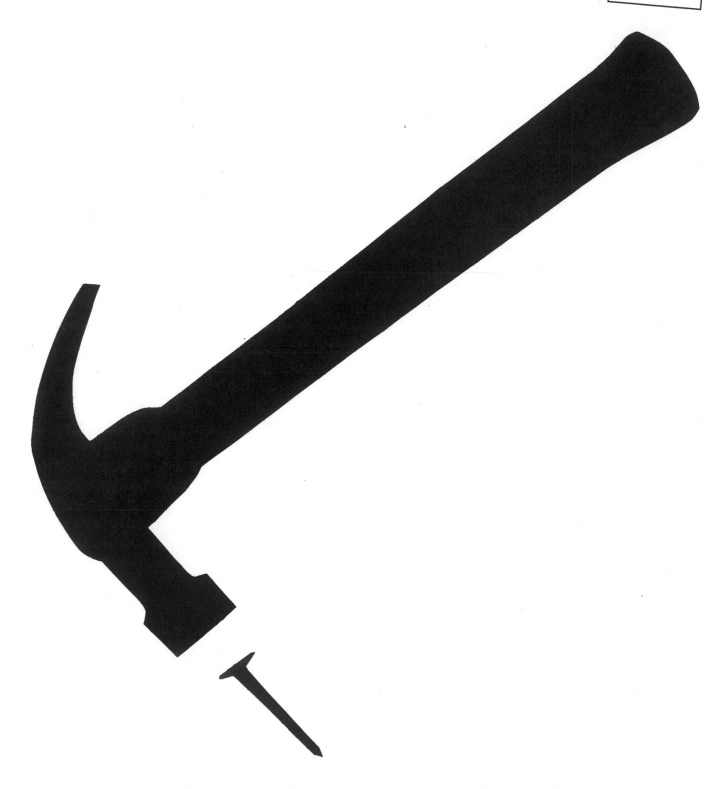

If my only tool is a hammer, everything becomes a nail.

12
Substitution

Objective

To use the strong metaphor of substitution of players in a sports team as a way for team members to define or validate "the numbers that count."

Procedure

At a team meeting, ask team members by a show of hands how many are involved in sports teams, either as players, spectators, fans, or as parents or friends of players. Group the team according to the kinds of sports with which they are associated: Soccer players over here, bowlers here, swimmers here, baseball players here, basketball players here, etc. Put any singletons together in a group. Have them get up and move their seats to be with others in their sport.

Ask the sport groups to discuss among themselves what makes a valuable player in this sport, that is, what kind of player would most typically get the "Most Valuable Player" award at the end of the season. Share the responses with the whole team.

Then ask each sport group to adopt the perspective of the coach who's responsible for training the entire team. Ask them to suggest a few guidelines for making substitutions, keeping in mind that team training is what coaches do, and that adding value to the game is a coach's responsibility. Share these responses with the whole team.

Then ask the team as a whole to apply these sports metaphors to the work of their own team.

Discussion Questions

Ask team members to define the value-added areas of the team's business, and what it takes to qualify as a "Most Valuable Player" on this team. Talk about the concept of substitutions at work, as learning opportunities and as ways to move projects forward, adding value in the process. Discuss the measure of "revenue per employee" and how that might

Notes

find a metaphor in points per player per game. Talk about what numbers actually count in this business, and whether or not the team is operating in a way that is consistent with such a measure. Try to get the team to define what the measures of valuable performance are, and, most importantly, to assess whether or not they're on the track to valuable performance.

I recently watched my daughter and son-in-law coach a co-ed basketball team of nine- and ten-year-olds learning to play for the first time. In true American kid fashion, the boys and girls on the team wanted most of all to score—to get the ball through the hoop by themselves and be heroes. It took a lot of coaching ingenuity, support, and teaching for these kids to play together for the team. Substitution of players was a key strategy for success. Teams at work could learn some lessons from the "Windsor Bus" team in Vernon, Connecticut!

Materials

None.

Approximate Time Required

20–40 minutes.

13
Reality Check

Objective

To "surface" team members' mental states at the beginning of a team meeting; to begin a team meeting from a baseline of reality and empathic understanding.

Procedure

Before the business of the meeting begins, simply go around the table, one by one, asking for a reality check on each team member's mental state. One's immediate "mental state" is often easier to describe than one's more deep-seated and complex "mental model," but often it sheds important light on an individual's probable approach to work in the hours ahead.

Start off with your own reality check. It might go something like this: "I've been up all night with my three-year-old who has the flu. I'm tired, grumpy, and not too fast on my feet yet. Please give me until noon to get my act together." The aim is to get each person to say how he or she feels (e.g., tired, grumpy, at loose ends).

If team members can describe the context and reasons for their mental states, but neglect to say how they feel, direct their thinking toward emotions. Expect a range of various key emotions: anger, sadness, fear, shame, disgust, surprise, love, and enjoyment are the main categories, with numerous variants within each. The aim of the exercise is to demonstrate to the team that emotions matter; they affect motivation, action, and achievement.

Discussion Questions

Facilitate a discussion about the role of emotions in performance. Focus on performance today. Encourage mutual support and working together through each other. Set reasonable, reality-based work objectives for the day.

Notes

Workplaces of yesterday rarely cared about anyone's emotional state, except perhaps that of a deranged misfit. In today's team-based workplaces, we've learned that emotions matter a great deal. In fact, Daniel Goleman, author of the book *Emotional Intelligence* (New York: Bantam Books, 1995), was a keynote speaker at the 1997 International Conference in Washington, DC of the American Society for Training and Development (ASTD).

Our mental states are capable of influencing a host of work-related behaviors and learning approaches: They affect what we notice or attend to, how available our memories are, the speed with which we process information and make meaningful connections, our ability to be assertive, our tolerance of ambiguity, and our sense of self-worth, just to name a few. Denying emotional reality seriously cripples the work of teams.

Materials

None.

Approximate Time Required

10–15 minutes.

14
Milestones

Objective

To involve the team in diversity planning.

Procedure

Meet in a room with a whiteboard that stretches across the front of the room. Across the bottom (at least 5 feet of whiteboard) draw a timeline representing the next 12 months. Segment the timeline into quarters, for example:

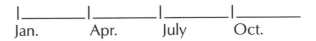

|_____|_____|_____|_____
Jan.   Apr.   July   Oct.

This is a first step in planning, a general overview, particularly appropriate for a team that has not had much experience in planning. The aim is to get the team to think about general areas of managing diversity for a 12-month period, starting now.

Break the team into small groups of 2 or 3 persons. Give each small group a 3×3-inch pad of self-stick notes that have been custom printed (or hand drawn by your staff) with the "milestone" image found on page 45. Each small group's task is to identify the types of things that should be done during the next year to truly honor, value, and manage the diverse workforce for the good of the business.

By using the image of the milestone, team members will be helped to think concretely about actions that can be measured. Before they go off in their small groups, talk a little about the idea of a milestone so that they begin to organize their thinking before they start actual planning.

Encourage the team to think of specific milestones for progress in many areas: career development, training content, training opportunities, communication within the company, external communications and public relations, partnering with schools and non-profit agencies, salary and performance reviews, re-

Notes

cruiting, staffing, internal mobility and flexibility, work design, home and family issues, benefits, rewards and bonuses, corporate sponsored recreation and celebrations, and policies. Don't attempt to organize their thoughts any further than giving them suggestions like these for broad areas of concern.

Instruct them to think in terms of definition first, and then placement of the defined milestone along the timeline in a specific quarter.

Give the small groups about 20 minutes to work on identifying the diversity milestones, then reconvene the entire team. Gather everyone in front of the whiteboard timeline and ask them to place their milestones above the timeline at the appropriate spot. Keep the action and commentary going as long as it is productive. Look for similarities and group milestones together with agreement from those who created them. Record the finished product on paper, and begin detailed planning soon thereafter.

Discussion Questions

Send the small groups off to their task with the question,

"What do we need to do, by when, in order to maximize the financial return to our business of our diverse workforce?"

> Make it clear that diversity is not some feel-good kind of thing we're dealing with, nor is it just a legal issue: Maximizing the benefits of a diverse workforce simply makes good business sense as the demographics of the labor pool change and as the markets for products and services become more diverse. Most people currently at work think of diversity as either or both of the former, that is, the purely human characterization or the purely legal definition. People need help thinking of managing diversity as a powerful tool for business success.

Materials

A stack of preprinted 3×3-inch self-stick notes and a marking pen for each team member; a room with a whiteboard stretching across the front.

Approximate Time Required

45–60 minutes.

Milestones

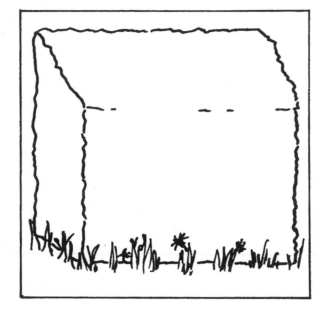

15

Diversity Range Finder

Objective

To get team members' votes on where the leverage points are for achieving successful diversity management targets.

Procedure

Use the chart on page 49 as a handout for each team member and draw it on a flip chart or whiteboard. Team members, one by one, will cast their votes for pressure points along a range of "more to less" in several previously identified diversity focuses. The ones on page 49 are examples; add your own to the list or change it to reflect your particular areas of concern.

Each person must stand up and be counted; each person's opinion counts equally. This kind of exercise makes certain that each one will be represented in the total.

Give the team a few minutes to study the handout and see the scope of the exercise. Together fill out the project or department name(s) on which they will be voting. There should be one handout for each project on which they will vote. That is, each team member may have more than one copy of the handout, depending on how many departments or projects you will be assessing.

Start the process of identifying the pressure points by asking the members of the team to answer this question:

> *"In order for diversity to be a strategic opportunity in this company, I'd exert this much pressure at this point _____."*

Each person is allowed one vote per line (category of influence). Each team member votes by placing an "X" on the chart according to his or her best judgment. After all have voted using the handout, tally the team's votes by having team members stand up to be counted. Record on the flip chart all number ones first, then number twos,

Notes

and so forth. Do the tallying in silence, going around the room systematically to collect all votes.

At the end of the voting and tallying, you'll see clusters of votes. At this point, open a discussion about why the votes were cast as they were. Continue as long as the dialogue is productive and until each person has had a chance to promote or defend his or her votes. Get general consensus on next steps to take in order to strategically maximize the opportunities in a diverse workforce.

Discussion Questions

Discussion can be expected to be somewhat tentative at first, because people are uncomfortable about possibly exposing their biases and "programmed" responses. The crutch of a specific vote helps people get started with an explanation, leading them into discovery of the "whys" behind the voting. It generally helps others to see all votes together, so no one is hanging out there alone. Keep after the shy team members: Begin with asking them to "describe" their votes; then "explain" their votes; then "defend" and "evaluate" their votes in relationship to others' votes. Describing is the easiest and most nonthreatening thing to ask of a reluctant participant. Focus on hearing from each team member; this is a lesson in participation and inclusiveness—one of the keys to successful diversity management.

> Two of the best books on the subject are by R. Roosevelt Thomas, Jr. of Morehouse College, Atlanta, Georgia. They are: *Beyond Race and Gender,* 1991, and *Redefining Diversity,* 1996. Both books are published by AMACOM, New York.

Materials

Diversity Range Finder handout for each team member (see page 49); whiteboard and markers.

Approximate Time Required

30–60 minutes.

Diversity Range Finder

Project/Department title: _____

Key question: *"In order for diversity to be a strategic opportunity in this company, I'd exert this much pressure at this point _____."*

	(more)	10	9	8	7	6	5	4	3	2	1 (less)
1. Communications											
2. Training											
3. Career Development											
4. Recruiting											
5. Motivation and Rewards											
6.											
7.											
8.											
9.											

16

What Did You Have to Leave at Home?

Objective

To help team members articulate the styles and patterns of talking that help or hinder relationships.

Procedure

This is an exercise in discovering the essentials of dialogue, a collective way of talking and interacting with each other that fosters organizational growth. The exercise is based on the principle of contrast: that is, a discovery of the power of seeing what something *is not* in order then to better see what it is.

The exercise is a thinking exercise, but may benefit from having someone act as a recorder at a whiteboard or flip chart for all to be able to see individuals' responses.

Simply introduce the topic of "talking" in the workplace. Focus the team's attention on the possibility that workplace talking has certain conventions, prohibitions, and styles unique to the present company culture. Talking includes memo writing and online talk through chat groups and e-mail as well as all face-to-face talking.

Then ask the team to think about the kind of talk they do at home, within the family, with friends, and in trusting and caring situations outside of work. Ask them to focus on differentiating the kinds of "home" talk. Ask them to be prepared to answer a question about the kinds of talk they left at home.

Go around the room, directing the following question to each team member in turn. Record responses for all to see.

> **"What did you have to leave at home?"**

Discussion Questions

By including the phrase "have to" in the question, you consciously set up the responder to draw a sharper contrast between home and work. Give cues to

Notes

what you're hoping to hear in their responses: for example, "admission of being tired," "freedom to laugh at somebody's really funny behavior," "asking for help—emotional and task-related," "telling someone they really messed up," etc. The list you get should be representative of ways people relate to each other in "safe" psychological situations.

Discussion following the listing should concentrate on types of talking that occur in such safe situations, at home and with friends. Ask if anyone can see any patterns in the list. Then digress into a discussion of workplace talk and how it differs. Begin by focusing on any area of patterns, contrasting those patterns with "home" talk patterns. Ask the team for concrete suggestions for making workplace talk more authentic, more related to what people need in order to develop and be productive both personally and organizationally.

Less hierarchy, empowerment, and team organization have all begun to create the need for different kinds of talking in our workplaces. As we are caught up in these changes, we often still operate according to the old, unwritten rules of corporate talking: promoting our own self-interest, covering our tracks, telling the boss what the boss wants to hear, limiting others' access to information and opinions, degrading others' points of view, etc.

Organization development guru Chris Argyris and his follower, Peter Senge, and others have written extensively about the importance of models of dialogue and human interrelationships. One particularly good summary of current thinking about dialogue is Nancy M. Dixon's *Perspectives on Dialogue*, Greensboro, NC: Center for Creative Leadership, 1996. Dixon's book is full of concrete suggestions about how to change one's workplace talking to facilitate organizational learning and personal development. It's a good book for your team reading list!

Materials

Whiteboard or flip chart and marker.

Approximate Time Required

10–30 minutes.

17
Good for Us!! ☆☆

Objective

To record one's own behavior toward mutual encouragement, or "promotive interaction" as Johnson and Johnson (1989) call it. To engage in self-assessment for a specified time period, e.g., 3 days, in support of specific other persons through structured types of dialogue.

Procedure

Set a time period for the assessment. Give each team member a Good for Us!! assessment checklist to use during this time period. Set a date for completion of the checklist, perhaps at a regular team meeting.

Review items 1 to 9 of the checklist, focusing on the kinds of intentional, structured talking that each item requires.

The objective here is to help individuals realize exactly how they are relating to other individuals through the "new" ways in which they speak with each other. Ask each team member to simply record a check mark in each column that applies to his or her own personal behavior through "promotive interaction," a particular kind of dialogue that consciously promotes the thinking and contributions of the other person.

As the check marks are entered, also enter the first name of the person to whom the "promotion" or support is directed, that is, with whom the interaction is experienced.

When the assessment records are brought together at the end of the assessment period, at the team meeting, ask team members to openly talk about the experience. Check to be sure that every member of the team is listed in the "With whom?" column. If there are omissions, determine why.

Discussion Questions

During discussion, ask team members to identify what they did that was different or new to them during these interactions, and to relate to the team what the other ("With whom") person did in

53

Notes

response. Talk about the possibilities for organizational—that is, team—learning through intentional dialogue.

Compare and contrast this kind of intentional and structured talk with other, perhaps more familiar, structured and intentional talk such as troubleshooting a plumbing or electrical problem, proving a hypothesis, brainstorming, saying a prayer, having a conference with your child's teacher, or deciding what clothes to take on a vacation. We talk in many kinds of structured ways to intellectually arrive at a specific outcome. These talking skills are learned by modeling others and by experience.

> David W. and Roger T. Johnson's book, *Cooperation and Competition: Theory and Research* (Edina, MN: Interaction Book Company, 1989), identified many variables associated with productive speech at work. Among their findings was the identification and elaboration of "promotive interaction," the subject of this exercise. Their work parallels the work of Chris Argyris in systems thinking and organization development. Such research into collaboration and cooperation is important to the more obvious structural changes of our workplaces, but it is also important to our quest for equal opportunity, fairness, and maximizing the benefits of a diverse and global workforce.

Materials

A Good for Us!! self-assessment form (page 55) for each team member.

Approximate Time Required

A few minutes' documentation time spread over 3 days, plus 15–20 minutes at a team meeting.

Good for Us!! ☆☆

Checklist for Actions That Demonstrate "Promotive Interaction"*

		With whom?
1. Provided efficient and effective help (timely, appropriate, so that the other could succeed)		
2. Exchanged needed information resources (no more, no less than needed)		
3. Provided feedback on the other's tasks and work responsibilities (for the other's benefit)		
4. Challenged another's reasoning or conclusions (to solidify his or her point of view and decision-making skill)		
5. Advocated mutually supportive action (to accomplish tasks together)		
6. Influenced another's efforts (to achieve mutually beneficial group goals)		
7. Acted in a trusting way (with or toward another)		
8. Was motivated by or motivated another (to work together on a challenging assignment)		
9. Kept anxiety and stress in check (so that another could function unhindered by anger or fear)		

*These 9 points of self-assessment are adapted from Johnson and Johnson, *Cooperation and Competition: Theory and Research,* Edina, MN: Interaction Book Company, 1989.

18
Outstanding!

Objective

To do an experiment in morale-boosting.

Procedure

Give team members the following instructions:

Go through the organization list for names that you recognize and randomly select 10 names. You will send a congratulations card to each person, knowing that you have no knowledge of anything particular about which they deserve congratulations. (Make the game more interesting by also repeating the experiment simultaneously with your personal mailing list such as a list of your aunts, uncles, and cousins, or your holiday card list. See if the personal list yields any more responses than the business list.)

The card should simply say on the front:

> **Congratulations!**
>
> **What a Great Job You Did!**

Sign the card "Sincerely," your name, organization location, and phone number.

Discussion Questions

The object of this little game is to see how many of the persons to whom you send the card respond to you in any way, especially to see if anyone was pleased to get the card for some honor or achievement. Psychological studies have shown that most people in fact do have something they're proud of and

Notes

do enjoy the boost in morale that comes from receiving a card acknowledging an achievement.

Ask team members to keep a log of responses, and compare them at a team meeting. Talk about ways in which to acknowledge others' achievements and build self-esteem.

> A very important foundation for organizational learning is self-esteem that comes from recognition without overt self-selling. This experiment should give the team some insight into issues of self-esteem.

Materials

10 or 20 blank cards, envelopes, and stamps per team member.

Approximate Time Required

30–60 minutes.

19

A Better Phone List

Objective

To personalize an organization's or team's telephone list.

Procedure

Work with the team to modify your organizational telephone list by eliminating last names. That is, personalize the list by listing each person alphabetically by first name followed by phone number and e-mail address. First names and e-mail addresses will give a surprisingly personalized "feel" to the list as last names are eliminated. The list should have entries like this:

Lisa	**8762**	**grankid@aol.com**
Carla	**9330**	**bestpen@aol.com**

Discussion Questions

Many companies, and teams especially, are always looking for ways to make people feel more noticed, more special, more empowered. Far-out and expensive "touchy-feely" experiential campouts and workshops, "be yourself" or "dress down" days, team slogans on T-shirts, vision quests, and "connecting" sessions are just a few of the recent attempts of people at work to tune in to their more private and personal selves. Caution against marketing at the expense of meaning.

Getting the message across that individuals count is sometimes a difficult sell in teamwork. Many approaches fail, including many of the approaches suggested above. The "Better Phone List" is a game with very little risk and often surprisingly good results.

Notes

> *The Witch Doctors,* by *Economist* staff editors John Micklethwait and Adrian Wooldridge (New York: Times Books/Random House, 1996) presents a rollicking overview of "management gurus" and what they perceive as the current, mostly sorry, state of management theory—an intellectual pursuit they characterize as being in its teenage years (pp. 323ff.). The book is a good review of empowering techniques and practices that worked, and that didn't work.

Materials

An old-style organizational telephone list, from which to make a new one.

Approximate Time Required

30 minutes.

20
Celebrate Success

Objective

To celebrate team successes by inviting another team to party with your team and informally share at least six team successes with each other.

Procedure

At some agreed-upon regular interval such as once a month or once a quarter, throw a team information-sharing party. Invite one other team, a different one each time, to join your team in the celebration.

Ask each team to bring evidence of at least three team successes (total of six) to the party. This evidence can be serious, frivolous, or symbolic—it can include costumes or musical accompaniment, songs, or dances. It should represent either a big or small but significant success that's worth sharing with another team for possible adaptation to other situations. Call on team representatives to present their success stories to the whole group, for celebration and applause.

Meet for two hours, one hour of which is company time (e.g., 4–5 p.m.) and one hour of which is employee time (e.g., 5–6 p.m.). Have music, balloons, table decorations, party favors for all, a master of ceremonies, food and drink, and maybe line dancing.

Discussion Questions

Ask who was involved in each success, how each person contributed to the success, and how the outcome for the team was possibly greater than the sum of the individual contributions. Applaud the individuals involved.

Notes

Celebrations are important because they demonstrate that the company cares about employees' contributions. Celebrations help teams feel united in purpose. Celebrations with sharing as part of them help engender enthusiasm and motivation for trying new things.

Materials

Party supplies, food and drink.

Approximate Time Required

2 hours plus a few hours' preparation time.

21
Guardian Angel

Objective

To engage in small acts of kindness toward teammates, either on the job or at home.

Procedure

Several team members, who tend to be the "social committee" type, get together and determine what kinds of nice things team members can do for each other. Some suggestions are: visit elderly or ill relatives under the care of a team member, bring food for the family during an illness, send birthday cards, give someone a ride to work, help a teammate's child with homework or a scouting project, give a teammate a helping hand with yard work or home improvement work, share a hobby with a teammate, help a teammate understand his or her personal computer better, etc.

After the list is generated, with many blank lines to add more topics, send it around to team members for them to check any topic(s) that they would like help with; that is, ask team members to ask for help in any topic listed or to add their own special topics. Collect the completed list.

Using the pattern on page 65 and your completed list as a guide, make a Guardian Angel for each person, naming the topic that person asked for. Make as many angels as you need to get all of the topics covered that were checked on the list. Each person may have more than one.

Cut out all of the angels, putting a string on each one for hanging.

Bring in a branch of a bush or small tree with many offshoot branches, and tie your angels onto the tree.

Bring the angel tree to a team meeting and explain the task ahead—that is, to support each other as human beings by choosing to be a Guardian Angel for someone on that tree. Ask each person to pick one angel from the tree by the end of the day and during the next week, execute or plan to execute the specified act of kindness toward a teammate.

Remove the angel tree to the team leader's office or a central place and encourage team members to visit the tree at their leisure before the end of the day. Don't make them choose in front of everyone. (Compensate for anyone who didn't get chosen by assigning that person to yourself or to another team member who you know will be able to address the need.)

Discussion Questions

At the team meeting explaining the Guardian Angel concept, focus on the universal human needs for belonging, for caring, and for help. The most successful teams are those whose members know each other very well and who truly care about supporting each other. Ask them if they thought they could be guardian angels—most people will say yes.

This exercise is adapted from the "Angel Tree," a holiday tradition at Church in the Gardens, Queens, New York. Thanks to Jeanne De Ycaza of the Adult Education Committee there.

Materials

Paper Guardian Angels (see page 65) for team members and a tree branch on which to hang them.

Approximate Time Required

60 minutes.

Guardian Angel

Monica

PC help

22
Free Lunch

Objective

To help solidify the employee/company integrity and trust bonds through a "menu approach" to employee perks.

Procedure

As part of your incentive program for employees, allow them to choose from a variety of company-related perks. Development of the menu is a typical and appropriate task for a team. If you are that kind of team, here's an update on an approach to the task. (If you are not that kind of team, be sure that your team has some input into the design of the perk menu.)

Adopt a perk design approach that promotes the company's products or services. It takes a bit more creative thinking than the typical "give-them-hockey-tickets" or "lunch-with-the-CEO" approach, but pays off in the long run in terms of company loyalty and goodwill. Here are some examples:

- If your company makes or sells cosmetics, let people choose a day at a spa, a gift certificate at the company store, or a facial at a salon of their choice.

- If your company is a beer or soft drink distributor, let people take home a case or two of their choice each month for a year, or allow them to have the company ship a case to a friend of the employee each month in the employee's name.

- If your company is part of the computer industry, let people choose gift certificates to Staples or Office Depot for computer gadgets, furniture, or software.

- If your company is in the entertainment or recreation business, let people choose tickets to sports events, concerts, dance performances, or plays; or arrange a donation in their name to any performing arts group or town recreation program.

Notes

- If your company is part of the health care industry, let people choose a gift certificate at their local pharmacy, several sessions with a personal trainer, a membership at their favorite health club, or karate, judo, t'ai chi, or yoga lessons.

Discussion Questions

Use your imagination and involve the team in the menu design. During the menu planning, ask repeatedly how the particular perk is related to the company's mission and vision of itself. Prod employees to think expansively; bring lots of choices to the menu. Be part of the *business system,* always.

Companies have offered employees perks for years. Among the common ones have been uniforms, breakfast, van pools, memberships in professional associations, lunch with the CEO, and tickets to local sports events. These are characterized by "one-way" flow, that is from the company downward—a control mentality. The idea is that this is what you need, or this is what's good for the company, so we'll give it to you. The newer approach recognizes that employees should be given choices, and that the menu from which they choose should support the company's reason for being.

Materials

A perks budget.

Approximate Time Required

An hour or so for planning.

23
More Honest Online

Objective

To define the nature of online communication; to set standards for online communication in support of the work of the team.

Procedure

Online communication has provided the environment not only for cross-functional teams within a company, but also for cross-continent teams across the globe. Much has been said in derision of electronic connections, particularly regarding how people write online, violating rules of grammar and social etiquette. People like to gripe about sloppiness and bad manners and say nasty things about what online communication is not. Lately, however, there have been some voices in support of online communications, particularly how it facilitates the work of geographically dispersed teams.

This exercise helps team members to establish standards for online communication by first taking a hard, analytical look at the nature of online communication. Start with an open discussion of the good things about online communication. Record brainstormed ideas on a whiteboard or flip chart for all to see. Expect things such as: candid, honest, fast, succinct, timely, direct, personal, etc.

Team members will be tempted to compare online with face-to-face communication and give responses like, "more candid," "more honest," "faster," etc. Try to get them to think only of the characteristics of online communication as they respond, not to simultaneously think of face-to-face communication.

Aim for a list of at least a dozen good things about electronic communication. Then ask team members to evaluate whether these characteristics describe a communication system that in fact is appropriate for the mission of this team.

At this point, it may be helpful to list the bad things about online communication and similarly evaluate whether these characteristics present insur-

Notes

mountable obstacles in terms of the team's mission, or whether and how they can be overcome. Record responses on another flip chart alongside the first one. Label the charts "good" and "bad."

Discussion Questions

Continue the exercise by facilitating a planning discussion about standards for online communication in this team. Refer to the team's goals or mission statement as you do this. Be sure that the good things are the primary focus; that is, accent the positive. The negatives ("bad" chart) usually fall in line if the positives ("good" chart) are the foundation for behavioral and usage standards.

> Communication systems within teams of all sorts and between teams and their stakeholders in and out of the company need attention. It is a grave mistake to assume that team members are communicating just because they suddenly are empowered to make decisions or are chummily thrust together in wall-less workspaces. New working relationships require new communication systems and patterns. It's a good idea from time to time to analyze how teams are communicating. This is one such analysis exercise.

Materials

2 flip charts and markers.

Approximate Time Required

30–60 minutes.

24

Create a Monster

Objective

To create a paper monster personifying ways in which a company destroys employee loyalty.

Procedure

This creative game is appropriate at a team-building workshop in which participants are not members of the same team. It is also appropriate for use with a team that's been around for awhile, at a workshop or team meeting. If you use it within a team, personalize the company to their company, not just "a" company.

Participants sit around a table or tables. Each table should have no more than 6 persons and no fewer than 3 persons. On each table are placed:

- a pack of multicolored 12×18-inch sheets of construction paper

- tape

- several pairs of scissors

- broad tip and medium tip markers in several colors

Introduce the topic of employee loyalty and facilitate a discussion about current events that show how companies "shoot themselves in the foot" and destroy employee loyalty. Cut off discussion before it degenerates into a gripe session, and direct the team's attention to the art supplies in front of them. Explain that during the next 15 minutes each table will create from these materials a monster that personifies how companies destroy employee loyalty.

The only ground rules are that each monster should have a head, a torso, arms, and legs. If the group is having trouble getting started, give them a suggestion or two. For example: "I think I'd make a monster with a forked tongue with the words *job security* written on it," or "My monster would have a swelled head representing executive pay, with dollar signs for hair." Make it

Notes

clear that they can cut and paste, fold and illustrate in any way they choose. Body parts don't have to be in proportion; body parts can even be intentionally missing.

Discussion Questions

Encourage people to get their frustrations on the table through this expressive game of creating a monster. Often in team work, there's an underlying unease about working together for the good of the whole in a time of economic instability. People instinctively want to relate better to their colleagues at work, but they are frustrated and somewhat afraid to give up the individual quest for excellence and reward that has traditionally characterized American workplaces. Games like this allow those frustrations and fears to surface in a safe environment.

During discussion prior to the actual creation of the monster, keep ideas flowing so that everyone's major fears and frustrations are out on the table. Come armed with newspaper and magazine articles illustrating either how a company did a great thing for employee loyalty or how a company really messed up and destroyed employee loyalty. Draw out reluctant participants with live examples from the current business press.

> Some of the most often talked about ways in which companies unwittingly destroy employee loyalty are: give huge executive bonuses and hold the line on employee increases; think of an employee as a cost to be fit into an accounting formula; lay off huge groups of employees but hire back some of them on a per diem basis without benefits; change job titles and eliminate jobs in the name of reengineering or rightsizing; withhold information; talk empowerment but act like mob bosses; accept no blame or responsibility for business downturn; offer no outplacement services for laid-off employees; never think beyond the bottom line.

Materials

Art supplies for creating monsters; articles from current business publications.

Approximate Time Required

45–60 minutes.

25
Chill

Objective

To remind team members that "chilling out" is an important skill that must be practiced in order to work successfully in a team.

Procedure

Make a copy of the poster on page 75 for each team member. Early in the life of the team, distribute these for display at each person's workstation. Encourage frequent reference to the poster and its five subskills. Encourage each team member to add his or her own subskills.

Discussion Questions

At a team meeting, discuss the pitfalls of working styles. Point out that in the traditional style of working with its focus on individual contribution, reward, and tight-lipped obedience to the boss, the opportunities for employees to interact in disagreement are minimized.

In teamwork, however, it's different. Effective team functioning depends on the daily, and often minute-by-minute, give and take—"process"—of communication and overt mutual support. People's personalities clash, their differing senses of timing affect each other, and their varying tolerances for invasion of private space often get the team into trouble. Rubbing the "team genie" doesn't suddenly make team members into perfectly collaborative, humble, nice, supportive folks.

The "people skills" associated with working style must be practiced and learned. This poster is a reminder to do just that.

Notes

Many sources have been commenting lately about the increase in personal stress apparent in our society. Violence with guns is on an increase in our workplaces, schools, and neighborhoods. New ways of working that require the discipline of collaboration and support are hopeful developments that can perhaps counter the effects of societal stress and violence. One recent study by Accountemps in New York City indicated that executives were spending 18 percent of their time intervening in employee personality clashes, about twice the amount of time spent in similar intervention just ten years ago. Workers, particularly team workers, need to develop strong skills for appropriate ways to work in order for the promise of team structure to be realized. This poster is one step in such skill development.

Materials

A copy of the poster, Chill (page 75), for each team member.

Approximate Time Required

5–10 minutes to distribute the poster and talk about it.

Chill

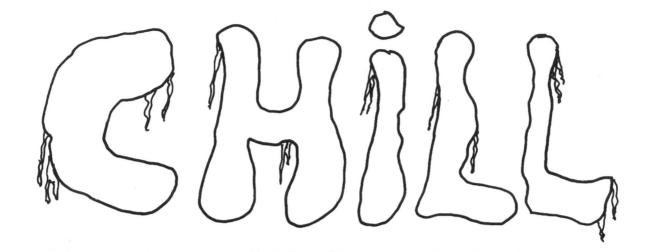

1. De-escalate.

2. Accept feedback.

3. Give feedback.

4. Modify processes.

5. Resolve emotional issues:
   fear, anger, frustration, loss.

6.

7.

8.

9.

10.

26
What Do You Feel?

Objective

To get the team to appreciate that each person is entitled to feel his or her own unique way; teamwork doesn't mean that everyone has to think and feel alike.

Procedure

Play short excerpts from five different pieces of music, each excerpt of the same time duration; for example, 1 to 2 minutes per excerpt. Choose five very different composing styles so that each excerpt sounds clearly distinct from the other.

Here are some possibilities: Aaron Copland, Indian pipe music, Chinese opera music, Johann Strauss waltz, English madrigal, Richard Wagner, J.S. Bach chorale, Widor organ music, Mozart string quartet, Alban Berg vocal music, rap music, country-western music, Gregorian chant. Make an audio tape of no more than 10 minutes and play the tape at the team meeting, pausing after each excerpt for writing.

At the end of each excerpt, ask participants to write down how they feel; that is, how the music makes them feel. Ask them to be as specific as possible, using differentiating terms such as outrage, hostility, exasperation, irritability, gloom, loneliness, grief, dejection, delight, amusement, friendliness, obsession, shock, wonder, aversion, hate, disgust, embarrassment, remorse. Encourage a range of responses.

Discussion Questions

After all five excerpts, open the discussion to compare and contrast everyone's responses. Simply ask what emotion(s) they were feeling with each kind of music. Value all responses; respect individual differences. Encourage self-awareness and acceptance of one's own perspective.

Notes

One of the best books on the subject of emotions is Daniel Goleman's *Emotional Intelligence*, NY: Bantam Books, 1995. In it, he makes the point that emotions come first, before cognition or thought, and that understanding emotions is critically important in today's fast-paced and changing workplace.

Materials

An audiotape of five different musical excerpts.

Approximate Time Required

20 minutes.

27
Which Mentor?

Objective

To differentiate among the different types of mentoring by having team members choose which kind of mentor they have been and which kind of mentor they would like to have.

Procedure

This is an action game in which participants move around the room according to their responses. Make six signs and place each in a different part of the room so that people can gather around a particular sign representing their chosen response. Signs can be laid on the floor or posted on a wall. The signs should say:

Counselor

Teacher

Sponsor

Protector

Rescuer

Oracle

These roles represent the most common types of mentors.

As the game begins, ask participants to vote twice, once for the kind of mentor they have been (those who have never been mentors may sit down), and once for the kind of mentor they would like to have for themselves (those who don't want a mentor may sit down). Ask the questions one at a time, letting people move to the sign that matches their choices.

> **"What kind of mentor have you been?"**

> **"What kind of mentor would you like to have?"**

Discussion Questions

After each movement around the room, discuss the various roles of mentoring, making the point always that the goal of such roles is to manage a diverse workforce, not to "assimilate" persons with

Notes

diverse talents and needs. The role of any kind of mentor is to help make the culture of a company apparent, and to help the novice acquire skills that lead to his or her own excellent performance.

Mentors are often assigned to newcomers, especially to persons who have been traditionally limited from access to promotion and other opportunities. Women and members of racial and ethnic minorities are commonly assigned mentors. Too often, mentors don't know what roles they are playing, are expected to play, or need to play. New team members, too, often are assigned mentors from among a pool of more experienced team members. Use this game to help clarify roles and expectations.

Materials

6 signs and tape to post them.

Approximate Time Required

20–30 minutes.

28
Bootlegging

Objective

To borrow the concept of "bootlegging" or "moonlighting" to introduce a new "inventiveness" policy that workers are expected to spend a portion of their time at work attending to their own inventions.

Procedure

This is a mind game of the fleeting sort that runs quickly through one's consciousness and helps a person internalize a new concept or practice. In this case, the connotations of bootlegging (a clever and risky practice) and moonlighting (holding two jobs) are both helpful instant organizers for the practice of encouraging employees to use work time and resources to spark individual creativity.

At the time of introduction of a serious policy such as that suggested in the objective, the use of such a mental organizer quickly provides a "frame" for thinking. Using words that conjure up strong mental images is a useful tool to help people reconcile seemingly conflicting messages in a new policy such as this. Simple reference to the policy as a kind of bootleg approach or a moonlighting by daylight can help.

Discussion Questions

Seriously used, verbal games such as this are valid tools for understanding. In this case, the message you want team members to hear is that it's okay to think about your own dreams and brainstorms on the job—that your work is the company's work, and that the company wants you to excel at what you're good at.

Notes

In order to implement an "inventiveness" policy, most companies set a percentage of time, such as 15 percent, and expect employees to follow the guideline. 3M company, for example, uses this as a conscious business strategy to bring new ideas to market faster.

Materials

A new policy statement, for discussion.

Approximate Time Required

10–15 minutes.

29
Card Deck Problem Identifier

Objective

To identify process problems as individuals and as a team.

Procedure

This exercise uses the conventions of a card game. Team members sit around a table, no more than 6 persons per table, as in a card game. If your team is larger than 6 persons, have more tables and run parallel games.

The essence of the game is that individuals vote by putting colored cards in the center of the table. Each color represents a value from 1 to 4, 1 being low and 4 being high.

Voting is done on a list of 10 common processes that must work effectively, efficiently, and importantly in order for teams to succeed. This game measures the team's opinion about how well each of these key processes is currently working. It is a snapshot of current opinion in order to correctly identify problems in team processes.

The variables of play are these:

> **red**   = **1 not at all**
> **yellow** = **2 somewhat**
> **blue**   = **3 to a large extent**
> **green** = **4 very much**
>
> **10 key team processes to be evaluated**
>
> **goal of "How are we doing at valuing people?"**
>
> **3 standards of team performance within each process: effectiveness, efficiency, importance**

Card patterns are on pages 86, 87, 88, and 89. Copy each of these pages onto corresponding colored paper and cut out the cards. Each person receives 30 red cards, 30 yellow cards, 30 blue cards, and 30 green cards.

Play begins with the instruction to vote your opinion about the team's perfor-

Notes

mance in each of the key processes against the overall team goal of "valuing people." Using the list of 10 processes on page 83, frame the question like this:

"This is a session on identifying problems in our current behavior on ten key processes as they relate to our overall goal of valuing people in this team.

(1) How **effectively** are we performing in the area of *setting objectives*? Lay out your cards in the center of the table. Then, how **efficiently** are we performing in the area of *setting objectives*? Lay out your cards. Then, how much **importance** do we assign to the area of *setting objectives*? Lay out your cards."

At the conclusion of voting on question 1, setting objectives, gather up all the cards and place them in a gallon-size sealable plastic bag and with a permanent marker, write on the bag, "1, Setting Objectives." Put it aside and continue in order through the list of 10 key processes, cueing the vote by asking the same kind of question as illustrated above. Bag all of the vote cards after each process and mark each bag.

Discussion Questions

After all 10 processes have been completed, spread the bags out and go for the ones with the most red and yellow cards in them. These represent the processes that need the most work. Use the bags as discussion-initiators. Ask the team which process they'd like to deal with first.

> The same content information can be obtained by a simple frequency count recorded on a whiteboard or flip chart, but overlaying the search for content with the elements of a card game adds a dimension of suspense, a heightened awareness of individual decision making, and a sense of the collegiality of the team.

Materials

Key processes chart, page 85; cards made from patterns on pages 86–89; 10 gallon-size sealable plastic bags; permanent marker.

Approximate Time Required

1 hour.

Key Processes for Team Success

1. Setting objectives

2. Sharing information

3. Making decisions

4. Dividing up the work

5. Doing the work

6. Evaluating performance

7. Planning

8. Having good meetings

9. Analyzing problems

10. Solving problems

Card Deck Red Page

(Each person needs 30 red cards: 10 effective, 10 efficient, and 10 important.
Copy this page 5 times to provide sufficient red cards for each person.)

effective

1 = not at all

efficient

1 = not at all

important

1 = not at all

effective

1 = not at all

efficient

1 = not at all

important

1 = not at all

Card Deck Yellow Page

(Each person needs 30 yellow cards: 10 effective, 10 efficient, and 10 important.
Copy this page 5 times to provide sufficient yellow cards for each person.)

effective

2 = somewhat

efficient

2 = somewhat

important

2 = somewhat

---

effective

2 = somewhat

efficient

2 = somewhat

important

2 = somewhat

Card Deck Blue Page

(Each person needs 30 blue cards: 10 effective, 10 efficient, and 10 important.
Copy this page 5 times to provide sufficient blue cards for each person.)

effective

3 = to a large extent

efficient

3 = to a large extent

important

3 = to a large extent

----

effective

3 = to a large extent

efficient

3 = to a large extent

important

3 = to a large extent

Card Deck Green Page

(Each person needs 30 green cards: 10 effective, 10 efficient, and 10 important.
Copy this page 5 times to provide sufficient green cards for each person.)

effective

4 = very much

efficient

4 = very much

important

4 = very much

---

effective

4 = very much

efficient

4 = very much

important

4 = very much

30

Human Factors Tally

Objective

To provide the team leader with a gut-level report on the team's successful implementation of six human factors that researchers deem critical for successful teamwork.

Procedure

Pass around a clipboard with the chart on page 93 on it at a team meeting. Do this regularly, for example, each week at the start of a meeting. List names down the side. Each team member puts a check mark in the column corresponding to successful implementation of each factor in his or her work this past week. (The exercise can be done also by focusing on the human factors that need improvement.)

The team leader can quickly see at a glance what's working, and by omission, see what probably needs improvement. Symbols aid in gut-level-type quick processing.

Discussion Questions

Use either the check marks or the lack of check marks to frame discussion of the essential human elements that the team is learning or must learn because it is a team. Contrast human factors with key processes (see page 85). This is not meant to be a carefully analyzed evaluation—it is purposely broad to elicit an intuitive or gut-level, quick response. Serious analysis follows this exercise.

Notes

> For a more extensive presentation of how human factors analysis can be used in teamwork and other participative work structures, see the case study of Hoechst Celanese presented at the International Conference on Work Teams sponsored by the University of North Texas Center for the Study of Work Teams, September 1996. The study is available through the Association for Manufacturing Excellence, Wheeling, IL, and appeared in its publication, *Target,* volume 11, number 6, as part of a longer article by Steven Cabana, pp. 16–30.

Materials

Chart on page 93, a pencil, and a clipboard.

Approximate Time Required

5–10 minutes

Human Factors Tally

CHART

team members' names	adequate elbow room	learning on the job	optimal variety	support and respect	meaning-ful work	a good future

SECTION TWO
Team Learning

Games Listed by Team Training Topic

Needs Analysis

32. Mapping How Things Are *101*
34. The Plagues of Hierarchy *107*
35. Valued Leader *109*
37. It's Not How Much You Know . . . *117*
38. Recipe for Success *119*
40. Business As U̲nusual *125*
43. Smoky Billows *133*
46. Not *the* Truth, But *My* Truth . . . *139*
49. Through the Looking Glass *147*
50. Left-Hand Column *149*
51. Upside and Downside *151*
52. White Space *153*
54. 80/20 and 50/5 . . . . *157*
55. Diamonds Are a Team's
     Best Friend *159*
61. Toy Box *177*
62. Discovering Digital Literacy . . . *179*
63. Daily Walk on the Web *183*

Improving Communication

39. Letter Bomb *123*
44. Listen Up *135*
45. Thinking about Thinking *137*
46. Not *the* Truth, But *My* Truth . . . *139*
47. Drafting the "Dialogue Bill
     of Rights" *141*
48. Say, What? *145*
50. Left-Hand Column *149*

Evaluation

34. The Plagues of Hierarchy *107*
35. Valued Leader *109*
41. Inquiry Skills *127*
49. Through the Looking Glass *147*
50. Left-Hand Column *149*
53. I Own This Business *155*
54. 80/20 and 50/5 . . . . *157*
56. It's a Numbers Game *161*
57. 360 Degrees Online *165*
58. Snow White and Grumpies *169*
59. Treasure Hunt *171*
60. 360-Degree Follow-Up *175*

Roles and Expectations

33. Plan-Do-Check-Act for Teams *103*
35. Valued Leader *109*
37. It's Not How Much You Know *117*
38. Recipe for Success *119*
47. Drafting the "Dialogue Bill of Rights" *141*
51. Upside and Downside *151*
53. I Own This Business *155*
60. 360-Degree Follow-Up *175*

Individualism within Teams

31. Upside-Down Training *97*
39. Letter Bomb *123*
43. Smoky Billows *133*
49. Through the Looking Glass *147*
53. I Own This Business *155*
60. 360-Degree Follow-Up *175*
61. Toy Box *177*
63. Daily Walk on the Web *183*

Problem Solving

39. Letter Bomb *123*
40. Business As _Unusual_ *125*
41. Inquiry Skills *127*
52. White Space *153*

Process Improvement

32. Mapping How Things Are *101*
33. Plan-Do-Check-Act for Teams *103*
41. Inquiry Skills *127*
42. Going to Grandma's *131*
45. Thinking about Thinking *137*
47. Drafting the "Dialogue Bill of Rights" *141*
48. Say, What? *145*
54. 80/20 and 50/5 . . . . *157*
55. Diamonds Are a Team's Best Friend *159*
60. 360-Degree Follow-Up *175*
61. Toy Box *177*
62. Discovering Digital Literacy *179*

Recognition

56. It's a Numbers Game *161*
59. Treasure Hunt *171*

Trust

34. The Plagues of Hierarchy *107*
36. Hat Trick *113*

31
Upside-Down Training

Objective

To illustrate a paradigm shift in training, by focusing on individual learning development within the team; to explore a model through which to design an individual learning development plan.

Procedure

Show team members the diagram on page 99. Explain that it is an inverted learning model, with the individual at the bottom. Ask team members to draw a similar inverted pyramid model on a piece of paper, without the labels, leaving enough space to identify learning needs in each level. Focus on the first three: "company," "department," "team." Reserve the "individual" for later.

The question they should answer is, "What are the key learning needs for this corporation, at company level, at department level, and at team level?" Ask team members to write down two or three responses per level. Go level by level, asking them to share their responses with the team before going on to the next level.

After discussing the learning needs of the team, continue on to the learning needs of the individual, urging personalized responses, that is, what each team member uniquely needs in the context of what the team needs.

A final step in this exercise is to begin to specify each team member's personal learning development plan for a 6-month or 12-month period.

Discussion Questions

Make the point that in teamwork, the training paradigm that focuses on what the individual needs to learn in order to fit into the organization is turned upside down. Rather, in team-based organization, it is the learning needs of the larger organization that must be brought to the level of the individual. Some thinkers call this "bringing the whole into the parts." It is a different way of approaching workplace learning from what we are used to.

Notes

Urge team members to conceptualize bringing down each level of learning need into the next lower level, ending with the individual level.

> Expect considerable discussion and some uneasiness about this model. Trainers especially are accustomed to thinking the opposite way, often seeming to be far away from corporate needs, often having no concept of learning needs of organizations. This is changing, however, as the artificiality of hierarchies is disappearing and empowered employees are beginning to act as if the business is their business. Along with this attitude change comes the need for conceptual crutches through which to understand the underpinnings of just-in-time learning, performance support systems, consultative training, and customized on-the-job learning. The individual's learning needs are critically important to trainers, but they must be met in the context of the whole. This model can facilitate a change in perspective.

Materials

Overhead transparency, page 99; overhead projector and screen.

Approximate Time Required

45–60 minutes.

Upside-Down Training

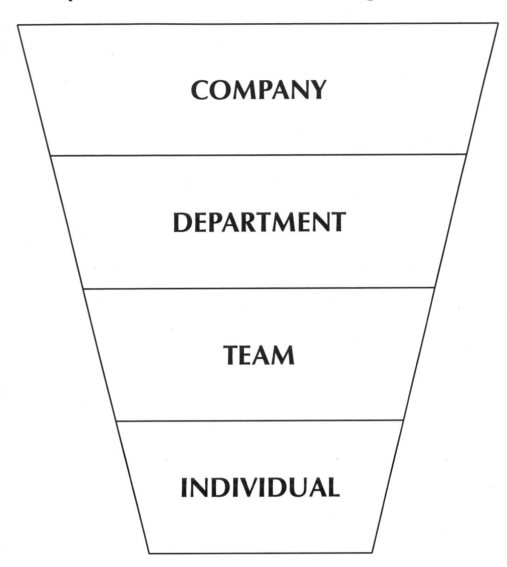

COMPANY

DEPARTMENT

TEAM

INDIVIDUAL

32 Mapping How Things Are

Objective

To map a work process in order to learn a technique for analysis of "how things are."

Procedure

This exercise is related to flow charting, a technique familiar to engineers, programmers, quality managers, and others. However, it starts with a more fluid and "chunk-like" approach to process definition.

Do this as a team exercise around a flip chart(s), whiteboard, or piece of newsprint spread out on a table. Involve the team members in interaction with each other as the spirit moves them. Don't make any attempt to keep it an orderly process—it should resemble brainstorming, with each person having a marker and encouragement to use it at any time to add to the "map."

Choose a process as a sample to practice the mapping technique. Examples are: getting lunch in the company cafeteria, parking the car in the company lot, asking for help from the computer hot line/help line, balancing your checkbook, making a turkey club sandwich.

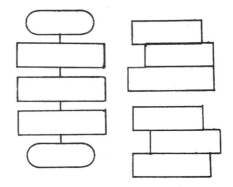

After the technique has been demonstrated and practiced, find an important work process to map using similar thinking and procedures.

Mapping works like this: Down the left side of the page, break the process down into its essential processes, much as you would think of a cross-country trip, going from Philadelphia through Columbus through Chicago through Omaha through Denver through Salt

Notes

Lake City through Reno to San Francisco, the destination. "Philadelphia" and "San Francisco" each would be represented by an oval box, all other essential steps by rectangles. They would all be connected by a straight line running through them from top to bottom.

Now the fun begins. In the rest of the space on the mapping paper, draw clusters of rectangles representing groups of related processes that could enhance the essential process. Continuing the trip analogy, maybe a side trip to Gettysburg or Valley Forge outside of Philadelphia might be fun, or a trip to an Iowa farm, or a dip down to Las Vegas, or a rerouting through Vegas and Los Angeles after Reno.

Set the team the task of mapping an essential work process; then develop the nonessential but enhancing side processes.

Discussion Questions

Facilitate a discussion of "how things are"; that is, using the essentials map on the left, have the team verify that all the essential subprocesses are actually in place. Then look at the nonessentials: Sometimes nonessentials are in excess and are actually preventing the key processes from working in an optimal way. Sometimes mapping a nonessential into the essential process makes it work much better.

Keep focused on a description of "how things are," moving back and forth between the essentials and the nonessentials, identifying gaps, but always trying to verify the way things are actually operating. Only with a constant testing of reality is it possible to make meaningful changes.

A typical human response is to gripe about a present bad situation and extol the virtues of what should be. This is an exercise in holding back that focus on what should be; rather, it is a testing of reality, a way of learning to analyze more carefully.

Materials

A large surface for mapping; markers.

Approximate Time Required

30–40 minutes.

33
Plan-Do-Check-Act for Teams

Objective

To help team members adapt the familiar quality movement model of "plan-do-check-act" to the work of teams, as a model for team learning.

Procedure

At a team meeting, ask each team member to draw a large circle on a piece of paper. Tell them that they will be expected to place four points on this circle, generally corresponding to the plan-do-check-act cycle. They should label each point anything they choose, as long as each point corresponds to one of the four processes in the Shewhart/Deming cycle of plan-do-check-act.

Their labels may be creative or direct, original or copied, as long as they describe a learning process. Show them the chart on page 105, either as an overhead or copied onto a whiteboard or flip chart, to use for ideas. Suggest that each team member's circle be reflective of one's own view of how team learning should occur in this team. Ask each team member to give his or her circle a title.

After the drawing has been completed, ask everyone to share their circles with each other, holding up and explaining the papers one by one for all to see. If you want to extend the identification and explanation session, ask team members if they personally feel more comfortable working at one point or another around the circle, and why. Ask them how their models are especially good or appropriate for teams.

Discussion Questions

During the "show and tell" time, refer the team to the work of Dewey, Shewhart, Deming, Handy, Senge, and other organization development thinkers. Suggest that the basic action-reflection learning paradigm is a strong framework for continuous learning that can be enhanced in numerous ways and adapted to the kinds of learning teams do best.

Notes

The trick, of course, is to alter behavior to match the espoused theory. This is the tough aspect of working in teams. Building in time for reflection and experimentation is the hopeful outcome of adopting a model such as this, getting the point across that each person (not just the R&D operation) is responsible for action *and reflection,* checking results, and connecting further action to planning. Teams are naturals when it comes to being able to implement this model that has worked so well in enhancing continuous quality improvement in product development. Successful teams are those that have been able to truly embrace the model and adapt it as a learning model to their unique business reason-for-being.

> Systems thinkers generally think in terms of circles, cycles, and loops—ways of approaching situations through mental analogies that tend to be circular in the sense that key processes move along into each other, like a circle, to keep the whole thing going. Walter Shewhart and W. Edwards Deming popularized the plan-do-check-act cycle for building quality into work processes. Their thinking is related conceptually to that of educational philosopher John Dewey, whose ideas are the foundation of the action-reflection way of learning. British management guru Charles Handy adapted this model into a "learning wheel"; systems guru Peter Senge and his followers further enhanced the learning wheel with particular adaptations to team learning. It is this last adaptation that is the foundation for this exercise. See Senge, et. al., *The Fifth Discipline Fieldbook,* NY: Currency/Doubleday, 1994, pp. 59–65. See also Handy, *The Age of Unreason,* Boston: Harvard Business School Press, 1990.

Materials

Chart on page 105 reproduced for all to see; paper and pencil or marker for each team member.

Approximate Time Required

1 hour.

Plan-Do-Check-Act for Teams

Shewhart/Deming	Charles Handy	Innovation Associates (Senge)
Plan	Decide	Joint Planning
Do	Do	Coordinated Action
Check	Reflect	Public Reflection
Act	Connect	Shared Meaning

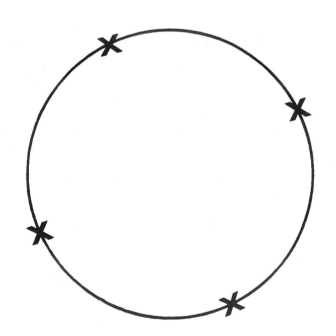

34

The Plagues of Hierarchy

Objective

To model reflective team behavior in a discussion about the obstructions to learning inherent in hierarchical organizations.

Procedure

This exercise requires honesty and the ability to maintain confidentiality. It should be done at a time when team members are ready to constructively criticize hierarchical organization, including the hierarchies that they might have created. Do this in a room where the door can be closed for privacy.

Begin with a simple, direct question to each assembled team member: "Are you in the right frame of mind to give constructive criticism?" If you get any no's for answers, excuse the naysayer from the meeting or ask him or her to stay but be a silent observer to the discussion following.

Seek information from each team member about the pitfalls and obstacles to his or her own learning in hierarchical organizations. Then ask the same question regarding the plagues of hierarchy that kill team learning. Attempt to group the responses in some way that makes sense, pointing out patterns of problems.

The goal of the exercise is to engage the entire team in group reflective activity, going back and forth using description, explanation, contrast, example, analogy, and evaluative judgment. Exercise these various cognitive thinking tools and means of verbal expression. An outcome of the exercise could easily be a statement of team values, as a result of clarifying what the team does not want to replicate from the hierarchical organization. Steer the discussion in the direction of values definition—it makes a very satisfying conclusion to a freewheeling feedback session. Make notes on a whiteboard or flip chart for all to see.

Notes

Discussion Questions

This kind of exercise is often part of a larger workshop in discovering one's mental models or identifying the larger system or organizational archetypes. The process of feedback used here is based on the technique of focusing on what's bad in order to discover what can be good. Like all "opposites" exercises, it is a way to solidify in one's mind what the impediments to progress are, making the way clear to define and commit to a better way of doing things.

During the discussion, ask team members to recall what people said or did to perpetuate the bad model, to "spread the plague," and how defensive routines and two-faced behaviors came into play. Ask them what values would have to be in place in order for things to change.

Another way to surface mental models and system archetypes is to engage in what has come to be known as "the left-hand column" exercise, developed by organization development guru Chris Argyris. It is built upon similar principles of comparison and contrast as in this "plagues" exercise. In it, a person writes a script down the right-hand side of a page (folded in half vertically) of how a particular problem was approached in a particularly poor and unproductive way. In the left-hand column, the person writes down how an honest, open, intellectually and organizationally free person would think. The writer tries to match styles of thinking across the page, decision by decision, situation by situation. This exercise should be done from the point of view of one and the same person, that is, how I actually behaved in a bad way versus what my inner "good" self was really thinking.

The "plagues" exercise has the added advantage that it can model effective team behavior through reflective team thinking, decision making, and problem identification.

Materials

Whiteboard or flip chart and marker.

Approximate Time Required

20–40 minutes.

35

Valued Leader

Objective

To define leadership, in a team context, through a "fill-in-the-blank" word game.

Procedure

Hand out a copy of the fill-in-the-blank description of leadership, page 111, to each team member. Ask them to focus on leadership; specifically, what it means to be a leader in the context of teams, and, of course, the context of their own team. That is, in the ideal, what are the value-added features of excellent team leaders?

In schoolteacher fashion, when they've finished, ask them to exchange papers, and one by one read the exchanged papers to the team. Come to consensus on the team's definition of a "Valued Leader." Write it down, copy it, and distribute it as a meeting follow-up for all team members.

Discussion Questions

Prior to handing out the leadership word game, compare and contrast various well-known leaders in business, sports, the arts, or public affairs. Ask questions about the value-added characteristics of those leaders that made them successful in their particular environment. Then ask team members to focus their thinking on the team environment and what its requirements are for leadership excellence.

Notes

This kind of word game is a break from the brainstorming type of exercises. This one features convergent thinking; the more open and free-wheeling discussion exercises feature divergent thinking. This exercise generally appeals to left-brained thinkers. It's useful as a quiet, solo exercise; and offers a contrast in style to the more noisy, shoulder-to-shoulder type exercises most frequently found in team meetings.

Materials

A copy of the Valued Leader fill-in-the-blank game (see page 111) for each team member; pencils.

Approximate Time Required

20–40 minutes.

Valued Leader Fill-in-the-Blank

Instructions: Please read through all of the items before filling in any blanks.

1. A team leader's power should come from _____

    _____

    _____

2. A team leader's effectiveness depends on _____

    _____

    _____

3. A team leader's worth to the company should be measured by _____

    _____

    _____

4. A team leader's task is to communicate _____

    _____

    _____

5. The best kinds of support a team leader can provide are _____

    _____

    _____

6. A team leader's commitment to the team is demonstrated by _____

    _____

    _____

7. The two most important roles a team leader should play are _____

    _____

    _____

8. The most perplexing paradox a team leader must cope with is _____

    _____

    _____

36
Hat Trick

Objective

To energize a meeting about how to build trust within a team or between a team and other organizations in the company.

Procedure

To play, you'll need a hat (as in a magician's hat—but a baseball cap will do, especially one with a team or company logo on it), and a bunch of rabbits (see pattern on page 115). Make one rabbit more than the number of team members, so that all players have a choice of rabbits to pull out of the hat.

Prepare the rabbits by writing one category of "trust busters" on each; that is, each rabbit should have a different category. If you have a large team, think of more categories or double up on some. Use the list on page 115 as a starter. Add as many categories as you can think of, or subdivide those listed to create more categories. Each should represent an area of company life in which there are often found obstacles to trust, "trustbusters."

Put all of the rabbits into the hat and shake them up. Send the hat around the table, high above heads so that no one can read what's on the rabbits. Instruct each team member to pull a rabbit out of the hat, look at the category, and answer three questions about trust

Notes

in that category. This can be done orally by going around the table from person to person, or it can be done through written responses first.

Discussion Questions

Ask if anyone needs further explanation or clarification after studying the category. The task then is for each person to figure out three things:

1. How trustbusters can be eliminated in that category.

2. How as an individual he or she can do something to build trust in that category.

3. His or her prescription for how the team can build trust in that category.

This game is designed to add a dimension of "lightness" to what is generally a "heavy" subject for teams—the subject of trust. Introducing this kind of dichotomy often helps people think more expansively and generate more ideas.

Materials

Paper rabbits and a hat from which to pull them (see pattern on page 115).

Approximate Time Required

15–30 minutes.

Hat Trick

Categories in which trustbusters are found:

support systems
information systems
recognition
rewards and perks
access patterns and privilege
standards of association
collaboration
communication
listening and feedback
quality improvement
skill development

37
It's Not How Much You Know ...

Objective

To design a team-focused criterion for hiring new employees.

Procedure

This is a team exercise, meant to involve the entire team in design of a new interview criterion to be used with potential employees who most likely will be assigned to work in a team.

Focus the team members' thinking by repeating, with a twinkle in your eye, the old saying,

"It's not how much you know, but ..."

Team members will be tempted to finish the sentence with the "business as usual" sarcastic ending, "... who you know." If they do this, laugh it off and say, "Not quite. It's a new world around here. The new ending to the sentence is:

"... how you learn."

Now that you have their attention, facilitate a discussion of what a new hire needs to be able to do at this company in a team. Get as many ideas out on the table as you can; turn the ideas into skills or areas of competence required for teamwork at this company. Then group the skills by weight—the most important ones first. Make your list sound like a typical help wanted ad (for teams), but add to it what you believe are the *associated kinds of learning* that are required for each skill. Here are a few to use as examples to get the team started:

technological literacy
troubleshooting, self-assessment, logical thinking

systems thinking
analysis, cause and effect, metacognitive skills

facilitation skills
communication, negotiation, divergent thinking

Notes

Establish a list of team success factors and pass on the list to your personnel recruiters.

Discussion Questions

Ask the team to identify the broad categories of experience and personality that augur success as a team member. Be sure that the team's responses fit into these categories; verify this with the team, and make modifications based on their responses. Ask someone to be a recorder during the discussion of responses.

Now that teams have been around for awhile, team members have a pretty good idea of what it takes to be a successful team member. These folks need to be asked what it takes, and their responses need to become a permanent part of the structured employment interview. This exercise can help provide a valid base of information.

Materials

Whiteboard or flip chart; markers.

Approximate Time Required

20–40 minutes.

38
Recipe for Success

Objective

To provide a lighthearted break in serious planning or visioning through the game of creating a recipe.

Procedure

At a workshop or team meeting, hand out a blank recipe card to each team member (see pattern on page 121). Place an extra stack of blank recipe cards in the center of the table in case anyone makes a mistake and wants to start over, or in case anyone wants to create more than one recipe.

Instruct team members to make up a recipe for team success as they have experienced it—their very best "family secret" type recipe. Remind them that a recipe has two parts, an "ingredients" section and a "process" section.

Ask them to fill in their names in the appropriate places on the cards, and when they're finished to share their cards around the table. Ask for volunteers to read some cards aloud so the whole team can hear and enjoy.

Discussion Questions

If team members are having a hard time getting started, give them some clues. Here are some typical ingredients: trust, ownership, empowerment, accountability, motivation, mutual encouragement, etc. Here are some typical processes:

- Mix thoroughly.
- Stir in.
- Chill.
- Keep at a warm temperature.
- Blend.
- Shape into.
- Discard.
- Wait.

Notes

Chances are you'll be amazed at what "gourmets" your team members can be! This is a quick and clever way to get people thinking about a team's vision and values. It's fun to do this at a workshop right before refreshments when people are starting to get a bit hungry. It's also fun to spread out the completed cards on the refreshments table during the break.

Materials

Blank recipe cards (from pattern on page 121) and pens or pencils.

Approximate Time Required

15–30 minutes.

Recipe for Success

Copy this blank recipe card, cut it out, and hand one to each team member to complete.

Recipe for Success

From the creative kitchen of _____

Ingredients:

Process:

39
Letter Bomb

Objective

To demonstrate that team learning can be better than individual learning.

Procedure

Buy 25 birthday cards, all about the same size. Fifteen of these cards should be the kind that have an electronic chip inside so that the card plays a song when it is opened. Buy these first, so that the other 10 cards can be about the same size. Stash the envelopes away; all you need for this game is the cards themselves.

Arrange the cards in 5 rows of 5 cards each, placing the musical cards randomly within the card matrix. The musical cards will be declared Letter Bombs. All other cards are safe.

X	X	X	X	X
X	X	X	X	X
X	X	X	X	X
X	X	X	X	X
X	X	X	X	X

The game can be played as a team if there are 6 or fewer persons on the team. However, the procedure that follows is for a larger team.

Divide the team into two subteams to encourage closer person-to-person communication. The object of the game is for each subteam to correctly identify—and ultimately avoid—the letter bombs.

The subteams work independently of each other, that is, only one subteam at a time is allowed at the table with the cards. (Send the other subteam into a far corner of the room or out for coffee while the first subteam is playing.)

Each member of the subteam gets one opportunity only to open all cards before the bombs are activated. All other subteam members must watch in silence as each takes a turn. When all of the

Notes

first subteam's members have taken a turn, send the subteam out to where the other subteam is waiting, and repeat the process with the second subteam.

After the second subteam has opened the cards, in silence, call the first subteam back around the table. Give the two subteams a few minutes to caucus within the subteams to decide which cards contain the bombs. It's okay if they want to replicate the 5×5 matrix on a piece of paper during caucus time as a cue card.

Each subteam should elect a representative to open the cards when the entire team gets back together. The final act of opening the cards should be done systematically, this time avoiding the cards with the bombs; that is, each subteam should aim to open the ten safe cards only.

Discussion Questions

Discussion after the game should focus on the power of collective learning. This is an exercise in performance; particularly, it is an exercise in the "discovery" part of the learning that leads up to successful performance. The point should be made that collective discovery has value that generally exceeds the value of individual discovery. Ask team members if they personally felt the increased power of team learning during the performance of the final task.

Psychologists for years have believed that an individual can remember about seven different items. Trainers who create overheads and slides, CBT screen designers, advertisers, and others have operated for decades according to this rule of seven. The Letter Bomb game tests this rule. It is one game that usually shows clearly the advantage of team learning.

Materials

25 birthday cards of about the same size, 15 of which contain electronic chips that play music when the card is opened.

Approximate Time Required

1 hour.

40

Business As Unusual

Objective

To articulate the stereotypes of "business as usual" in order to discover better models of learning and working.

Procedure

At a team meeting, ask team members to think of all the stereotypes of workplace behavior and unwritten rules of doing business in this company. The point is to get all of the "business as usual" stereotypes out in the open. This can be difficult for some folks who know of no other way of thinking. Expect stereotypes such as: cover your tail, keep your head down and mouth shut, play to the boss, ship it, look out for number one, I don't get paid to think, I just follow orders, give her the numbers she wants, etc.

Open a free-for-all call-out session, in which anyone can call out a pet stereotype. Keep it going as long as ideas keep coming. Choose a few of the stereotypes to focus on, writing each on a flip chart or whiteboard.

Discussion Questions

Now ask the team to suggest ways in which the stereotypes you've chosen can be broken. Keep discussion going—it's the discussion that's the valuable part of the exercise—jotting down synthesizing comments or key points next to the stereotypes in focus. At some point in the discussion, make the statement that one of the goals of the team must be to make team learning "generative" rather than "adaptive." Generative learning is the only way to manage business as <u>un</u>usual. The kinds of behavior that perpetuate the stereotypes are adaptive behaviors, doomed to failure as business changes.

Notes

> Peter Senge in *The Fifth Discipline* (NY: Doubleday/Currency, 1990) says that the unexamined models of thinking that drive behavior ("business as usual") severely limit an organization's range of actions to what is familiar and comfortable (pp. 186ff.). This exercise brings those models to the surface for serious scrutiny.

Materials

Flip chart or whiteboard and marker.

Approximate Time Required

20–30 minutes.

41
Inquiry Skills

Objective

To identify and practice various inquiry skills; upon reflection, to assess the presence or absence of inquiry skills in other team members.

Procedure

Do this reflective exercise at the end of a team meeting at which the team wrestled with a particularly knotty problem. Each team member will be responsible for reflecting upon the inquiry behavior demonstrated by two other team members. All team members will thus be reflected upon by two persons.

The reflective assessment will be focused by the Inquiry Skills Checklist on page 129. Make copies of this and hand out 2 checklists to each person. Fill in the team members' names ahead of time and be sure that no one gets himself or herself to assess.

When all checklists have been distributed, review the items on the checklist to be sure that all team members understand them. When all are focused and ready, ask each person to simply indicate with a check mark in the Yes or No column whether or not the person being assessed demonstrated that skill during the previous team meeting.

When all have finished the two checklists, call a team member's name and have the two persons who reflected upon that person's behavior read the check marks, making any additional observations that would clarify the assessment.

After all team members have been featured in the same manner, open discussion about how the No's could be changed to Yes's. Ask the team member, with the team's input, to suggest how he or she could have acted in order to turn any No responses into Yes responses. Have the team member devise a response that could qualify for a Yes check mark. Applaud that Yes response!

Notes

Discussion Questions

Ask individuals how they could have changed their thinking to be less aggressive, less withdrawn, or less an advocate for their own point of view at the expense of others' points of view.

There is no winner or loser here, so resist the temptation to add up the No responses of the poor folks who instinctively behave according to old models. The thing that gets the applause is correcting the No behaviors. Focus on that *process of correction,* not the column of check marks.

> The idea of learning new skills for interpersonal relationships is an important part of developing a team's capacity for continuous learning. Accepting and giving feedback, reflection, dialogue, and inquiry are just some of the new skills worth developing in depth. These skills come from an amalgam of sources in cognitive psychology, creativity literature, organization development, systems thinking, and philosophy.

Materials

2 Inquiry Skills Checklists for each person; pencils.

Approximate Time Required

1–1½ hours.

Inquiry Skills Checklist

Person being assessed: _____

Person filling out this checklist: _____

Instructions: Place a check mark in the appropriate column, indicating your assessment of this person's behavior on each of the inquiry skills.

	Yes	No
1. Ask questions honestly to seek an answer, not to show superiority.		
2. State and acknowledge your own assumptions.		
3. Use backup data to support your assumptions.		
4. Ask what the other person's assumptions are.		
5. Actively listen for the other person's response.		
6. Ask if there's another way to approach the problem.		
7. Ask for feedback on his or her own thinking.		
8. Ask for help.		

42
Going to Grandma's

Objective

To articulate a list of advocacy skills that are important in teamwork.

Procedure

This game is a take-off on the children's game (we used to play it in the car on a long trip), "Going to Grandma's." The idea of that game was to be sure to take to Grandma's all of the things that would make Grandma think (continue to think) you were the most wonderful person in the world. Each person in the car, in turn, would be allowed to add something to the list, but had to recite the entire list of everyone else's items before he or she could add an item. Whoever missed was out; the last person remaining was the winner. Typical items were: my report card, the mitten I knitted, my basketball trophy, Frisky's picture, my new glasses, etc. Play begins with, "I'm going to Grandma's and taking (A)." The next person says, "I'm going to Grandma's and taking (A) and (B)." The next person says, "I'm going to Grandma's and taking (A), (B), and (C)." And so the game continues until there's just one person left, clearly the one with the most goodies to take to Grandma's. Remind players of this children's game before you begin the analogy play with advocacy skills.

Talk a little about the necessity in teamwork for each person to be humbly assertive, that is, to develop and practice the skills of advocacy so that new ideas and strong ideas can be effectively incorporated into the work of the team. Ask the team what they think advocacy skills are. These are some possibilities:

Be logical.

Be clear.

Seek constructive criticism.

Accept another's perspective.

Facilitate seeking options.

Do your homework.

Notes

Load your brain with data.

Seek collaboration.

Each of these can be turned into an "item" to take to Grandma's: for example, logic, clarity, criticism, perspective, etc. Add as many others to the list as the team can think of.

Start by saying that we're all going to Grandma's with a set of advocacy skills.

Begin the game as if it were the children's game: "I'm going to Grandma's and taking _____." Continue the play as long as you can until you get a winner. If everyone falls out early, start the game again using a flip chart list of advocacy skills as a cue.

Discussion Questions

This game benefits from a discussion of the differences between aggression, assertiveness, and advocacy. In order for the productive work of teams—and continuous team learning—to take place, team members must learn to hone the positive skills of advocacy. This combination definition exercise and memory exercise, in the wrappings of a game, can help team members articulate a definition of advocacy and distinguish it from other, less positive skill sets.

This advocacy skills game and the previous exercise on inquiry skills are both ways to learn to identify a new set of skills. The traditional way of approaching the need to learn to identify sets of skills is to simply hand out a list of skills, or refer the team to a conference paper or video lecture about the skills. These two games illustrate participative approaches, both of which exercise the brain in different but equally important dimensions.

Materials

List of advocacy skills on a flip chart.

Approximate Time Required

20–40 minutes.

43

Smoky Billows

Objective

To use the image of smoke coming out of a chimney to encourage team members to appreciate the value of silence.

Procedure

Draw a billow of smoke coming out of a chimney, the way small children typically do. It's an image that suggests home, warmth, perhaps a gathering around a fireplace. Most people will relate to this image with a quiet smile. This is an exercise in experiencing the power of a simple image, and the experience begins with your drawing. Focus on the billowing smoke. Draw on a piece of paper, flip chart, or whiteboard so that all can see.

Imaging has been around a long time, and is useful in counseling, psychology, visual and performing arts, and writing. It has not been a standard tool in one's business management toolkit, but deserves a closer look at its potential usefulness as a learning tool for teams.

Ask team members to focus on the smoke, letting their minds wander back to their childhood days when they drew pictures like this. Ask them in silence to imagine a cozy gathering of friends or family around a fireplace. Ask them to remember colors or sounds that might have been associated with that fireplace. Ask them to be aware of the silence and its calming effect.

Notes

Then ask them to be aware of their own breathing, and to consciously take in longer, smoother breaths. Ask them to use this few minutes of silence to refresh their minds.

Discussion Questions

The kinds of questions raised or issues addressed after this exercise will depend on what occurred in the team before the exercise was started. If there had been particularly contentious debate or ineffective attempts at communication or problem solving, then plenty of questions about contrasting one's mental state "before" and "after" would be appropriate. If this exercise is presented as one in a series of tools for better team learning (for instance, games 41, 42, and 43), questions could focus on comparing and contrasting the methodologies. Team members could simply be encouraged to not be afraid to doodle, dream, take the time to be quiet, and allow their minds to be refreshed by silence.

Team members could be encouraged to gradually become aware of the silence of fellow team members too, in a kind of collective connection with each other within the positive memory of an image. You can extend the smoke image, suggesting that the trailing billows move gently upward, unconstrained by forces of anger or self-centeredness. Ask team members to silently consider what might have been changed for the team's previous meeting dynamics to be able to move unconstrained, like the smoky billows in their imagination.

> The magic in this "game" is its pure simplicity and usefulness in many situations. Many other images can be used; some common ones are: bubbles from a child's bubble wand, a flower opening, waves on the beach. The important outcome is to enable individuals to experience silence and realize its power for learning.

Materials

A surface upon which to draw a picture; marker.

Approximate Time Required

5–30 minutes.

44
Listen Up

Objective

To sensitize team members to the skill of active listening and to practice it.

Procedure

Seat team members close to each other in a circle, so that at least their chairs are touching—maybe their knees or ankles too. Pass around ski headbands (Polartec™ fabric or other nonallergenic material) for each team member to use during the exercise. These will be used as blindfolds, to wear around the forehead, covering the eyes. Ski headbands are best for the purpose of covering eyes because they are generally of thicker, more dense fabric than tennis or cosmetic stretch headbands.

The purpose of the blindfold is to eliminate the sense of sight in order to accentuate the effects of the sense of hearing.

Begin the exercise by asking all team members to cover their eyes with the headbands. Wait until all have done this and the agitation of the physical movements has stopped. Ask the team to feel the quiet atmosphere and to tune up their ears for hearing. It's time to Listen Up.

The "play" in this exercise is for the individuals in the circle to conduct a conversation about some real problem or issue in the team. Fewer customer complaints, shorter routes for paperwork, or better communication flow are just some of the typical topics that need to be talked about in teams. The point of the exercise is for individual team members to be acutely aware of what is being said, that is, to heighten their awareness of the contributions of others by listening.

You, the only sighted and hearing person, as team leader, trainer, or facilitator must keep the dialogue going until all participants have been engaged in listening. This is not an exercise in problem solving; it is an experience in active listening.

Notes

Discussion Questions

At the conclusion of the exercise, have team members remove their headbands and debrief the experience together. You will typically find that posturing ceases, showing off and acting superior doesn't work, and people say what they mean when they have to be heard only and not seen too. Suggest that they remember what this kind of honest conversation felt like, and try to use the skill of acute, active listening in all team conversations.

Like the other team learning skills in the three preceding games, active listening must be experienced, contrasted with traditional communication models in use, and practiced. Teams need to be reminded how it feels to communicate differently; they won't learn it by reading about it or seeing videos about it. Skills need visceral, physical involvement and practice.

Materials

A ski headband for each team member.

Approximate Time Required

20–40 minutes.

45

Thinking about Thinking

Objective

To engage the team in analysis of the process of discussion; to examine discussion as a learning tool.

Procedure

This is a good process with which to use the content of developing a mission statement or developing a project timeline. If these content areas are not relevant to your team, pick an area of content that has a fairly clear structure but is subject to many differing points of view to accurately and finally define it. This is an exercise not so much about content, however, as about process. Content here is the way into thinking about thinking.

Tell the team that the following exercise has a dual purpose: to ultimately design a finished "product," for example, a mission statement or a schedule, as well as, and more importantly, to analyze the process of discussion that led to the successful outcome. Ask the team to focus on discussion, the standard language tool of convergent thinkers who, in combination with others, pull together many separate ideas and turn them into a synthesis of all ideas.

Discussion, like percussion or concussion, features a breaking apart. Too often in our workplaces, the process stops there and the pieces are never picked up. Suggest to the team that this exercise will help them see the correct process of coming together after the natural breaking apart.

Identify discussion as an important foundation skill for teamwork. Suggest that it must be understood in order to be refined. Suggest that the metaphor of a political convention that follows can help team members see how discussion works.

Provide two runners, one on either side of the room, each of whom will serve about half of the team. (This is a good exercise for a larger team of 20 or more people.) Suggest the setting of a political convention or town meeting at

Notes

which members of the audience are directing questions or points of view to the candidate up front. Audience members have been requested to write their question on a card, shout out its main idea, and hand the card to the runner nearest them who will run it up the aisle to the candidate for a response. Many people speak up in order to be heard by the candidate, many defend their positions loudly by their words or actions, many are eager for the approval that comes when the candidate agrees with them.

Follow the same format, giving each team member a pad (or partial pad) of 3×5-inch self-stick notes. Play patriotic music in the background to set the stage for the political scene analogy, get the runners in place, and start the play. Ask team members, for example in developing a mission statement, to write down one thing to be sure to include, call it out, and hand the self-stick note to the runner.

The runner, as in a political event, takes the note, runs it down front, and posts it on a whiteboard. The game continues until all persons have been included. Many ideas per person are welcome. The runners then group the idea cards with similar ideas together, and the process of "picking up the pieces" begins.

Discussion Questions

The contribution of ideas via self-stick notes and their subsequent synthesis is an analog of the discussion process. Conclude the session with a discussion about discussion, and how to make it better for their team.

In business-as-usual workplaces, people don't pay much attention to how they think: Thinking about thinking is not high on anyone's priority list of ways to account for time at work. In teams committed to continuous learning, however, this should be different. Start the process by suggesting that there are at least three different ways to learn: spontaneously as things come up, unexpectedly as in a surprise conclusion or an accidental discovery, and intentional learning that has been planned and has expectations built into it. Ask the team members to give examples in these categories from their own experiences as learners. Set the stage for their thinking about discussion as a learning tool especially for teams.

Materials

3×5-inch self-stick notes for all; whiteboard and marker; music.

Approximate Time Required

30–60 minutes.

46
Not *the* Truth, But *My* Truth

Objective

To engage the team in understanding and use of the process of dialogue; to examine dialogue as a learning tool.

Find a current article in a business magazine or newspaper about some controversy (political fight, company problem, financial disaster, etc.) that team members will be interested in; make a copy for each and distribute this prior to a team meeting or training session, asking each person to read it.

At the meeting of the team, refer to the article. Tell the team that this exercise will use the article as a learning aid for the team to experience the discipline and value of dialogue. Identify dialogue as a partner to discussion, but different in its divergent thinking requirements.

In dialogue, ideas are not quickly separated apart as in discussion; they are instead more likely to be held in suspension and expanded. Dialogue depends on exploration and deep listening. If discussion is hot energy, then dialogue is cool energy. Dialogue continually moves outward; discussion ultimately moves inward. Help the team to understand these differences before the exercise begins.

The exercise requires the team to dialogue with each other about the article they have all read. As the team focuses on the task of answering the questions you pose about the article, guide their way of responding so that it approaches the model for dialogue. Stop responses that are clearly not dialogue; make corrections in process. Enlist the help of others who see the errors in expression. Help the team to experience the discipline of dialogue in this safe training setting. Try to get everyone into the process. Make the point that those in dialogue must acknowledge that their comments are their own truths, not the one and only ultimate truth. Dialoguers, those who engage in dialogue,

Notes

must be responsible for themselves and to themselves. In dialogue, there are no pretense, no posturing, no coverups. Dialogue is open to challenge in the name of finding better ideas. Dialogue is a great tool for team learning.

Discussion Questions

Lead the group into dialogue about the article around questions like these (adapt the questions to your particular article):

1. What is the main point of the article?

2. Who are the main actors?

3. What are the relevant characteristics of the main actors (ego flaws, poor decisions, the wrong mind-set, bad circumstances, the wrong friends, etc.)?

4. Why was this article written?

Two good books on the subject of dialogue are: *Perspectives on Dialogue* by Nancy M. Dixon, Greensboro, NC: The Center for Creative Leadership, 1996; and *The Fifth Discipline* by Peter Senge, NY: Doubleday/Currency, 1990, especially chapter 12, "Team Learning."

Materials

A copy of a recent article from a business magazine or newspaper for each team member to read ahead of the training session.

Approximate Time Required

1–2 hours.

47

Drafting the "Dialogue Bill of Rights"

Objective

To create a set of standards for dialogue among team members, using the United States of America's Bill of Rights as inspiration.

Procedure

After some experience with the study of dialogue, lead the team in creating its own standards for dialogue as they see it working for the good of this team. Focus on the process of drafting the document; encourage team members to model the dialogue process as they engage in the task.

Use the Bill of Rights, the first ten amendments to the Constitution, (reproduced on page 143) for inspiration. Make a copy for each team member to use during the exercise. Talk a bit about the inspiration for the Bill of Rights, and perhaps quote a few lines from the Preamble to the Constitution (1789):

"We the people of the United States, in order to form a more perfect union, establish justice, insure domestic tranquility, provide for the common defense, promote the general welfare, and secure the blessings of liberty to ourselves and our posterity, do ordain and establish this Constitution for the United States of America."

The company's mission statement can also be used, in parallel with the Preamble, to indicate the thinking that drives the creation of standards of behavior at work and of laws of civil society. Quickly review the ten key ideas in the Bill of Rights, noting the behaviors written into each amendment.

Suggest that the team reflect on what they have learned about dialogue and about specifics of their own individual and team attempts to use it as a tool for continued learning. Ask team members to talk out loud as they organize their thoughts about dialogue. After several good ideas have surfaced, move the exercise into the creation of their own standards for the practice of dialogue.

Notes

Ask someone to record the responses on a flip chart, leaving plenty of space for rewording and refining of concepts.

Discussion Questions

Ask the question, "What standards will we adopt in our use of dialogue for the work of this team?" Here are some common ones; start the group off with a suggestion or two. Facilitate deeper explanations that suggest the direction of appropriate behavior.

> *Suspend judgment. Explore alternative paths. Talk from the center outward. Be prepared. Accept the points of view of others. Seek to understand. Raise issues. Voice another's opinion.*

Refer to the Bill of Rights for ways of using language. Try for at least five standards, but probably no more than ten items.

Dialogue is a creative tool; this exercise models the creative process of dialogue in creating the team's personalized and customized standards document. Be sure that each team member gets a copy of the finished document.

Materials

A copy of the Bill of Rights (see page 143) for each team member; flip chart and markers; pencils and paper.

Approximate Time Required

30–60 minutes.

The Bill of Rights

Amendments 1 - 10 of the United States of America's Constitution (1791)

1   Congress shall make no law respecting an establishment of religion, or prohibiting the free exercise thereof; or abridging the freedom of speech, or of the press; or the right of the people peaceably to assemble, and to petition the Government for a redress of grievances.

2   A Well regulated Militia, being necessary to the security of a free State, the right of the people to keep and bear Arms, shall not be infringed.

3   No Soldier shall, in time of peace be quartered in any house, without the consent of the Owner, nor in time of war, but in a manner to be prescribed by law.

4   The right of the people to be secure in their persons, houses, papers, and effects, against unreasonable searches and seizures, shall not be violated, and no Warrants shall issue, but upon probable cause, supported by Oath or affirmation, and particularly describing the place to be searched, and the persons or things to be seized.

5   No person shall be held to answer for a capital, or otherwise infamous crime, unless on a presentment or indictment of a Grand Jury, except in cases arising in the land or naval forces, or in the Militia, when in actual service in time of War or public danger; nor shall any person be subject for the same offence to be twice put in jeopardy of life or limb; nor shall be compelled in any Criminal case to be a witness against himself, nor be deprived of life, liberty, or property, without due process of law; nor shall private property be taken for public use, without just compensation.

6   In all criminal prosecutions, the accused shall enjoy the right to a speedy and public trial, by an impartial jury of the State and district wherein the crime shall have been committed, which district shall have been previously ascertained by law, and to be informed of the nature and cause of the accusation; to be confronted with the witnesses against him; to have compulsory process for obtaining Witnesses in this favor, and to have the Assistance of Counsel for this defence.

7   In suits at common law, where the value in controversy shall exceed twenty dollars, the right of trial by jury shall be preserved, and no fact tried by a jury shall be otherwise re-examined in any Court of the United States, than according to the rules of the common law.

8   Excessive bail shall not be required, nor excessive fines imposed, nor cruel and unusual punishments be inflicted.

9   The enumeration in the Constitution, of certain rights, shall not be construed to deny or disparage others retained by the people.

10   The powers not delegated to the United States, by the Constitution, nor prohibited by it to the States, are reserved to the States respectively or to the people.

48
Say, What?

Objective

To practice one technique of dialogue.

Procedure

At a team meeting or training session, choose a topic that often gets everyone hot under the collar, for example:

1. Who should call the shots, marketing or R&D?

2. What's a reasonable rate of customer returns?

3. How much quality loss can we still ship?

4. What should we be paying for consultants?

5. How much inventory is too little/too much?

6. Who deserves/needs a company car? A driver?

Tell the team that for the next few minutes, they should tackle the issues involved in the topic. Ask them to interact with each other in a manner that they consider dialogue, as contrasted with discussion. Suggest that in dialogue, (A) remarks should be made in a spirit of open inquiry, not defensive advocacy; (B) assumptions should be stated, supported, and challenged; and (C) ideas should flow without regard to one's place on the organization chart or salary level.

Let the dialogue begin, with these three (A,B,C) suggestions in mind. Keep the talk going until it reaches a lively point, then stop it, remembering some key words in the dialogue so that you can facilitate a resumption of it in a few minutes.

Now introduce the following technique, simply known as the "Say, What?" technique.

The Say What? technique works like this: Move conversation forward into di-

Notes

alogue by using language that clarifies. The easiest way to do this is to ask a question with the word "What?" in it. In this way, the speaker expects and seeks a specific answer. Another way to think about this is to think about seeking a noun response. Here are examples: "What leads you to say this?" "What makes you ask?" "What do you really believe?" "What bothers you about what I said?", etc.

Pick up the dialogue where it left off before introduction of the Say, What? technique. Facilitate a practice session as the dialogue continues, so that each team member has a chance to use the Say, What? technique.

Discussion Questions

Ask the team to debrief their dialogue session. Ask them first to focus on the process of talking, then to focus on the nature of the content or depth of issues. Ask them if they were aware of using a structured approach to talking. Ask how they thought such an approach affected the content.

Ask them for suggestions for improving their dialogue.

> Far too many people at work see work as a winner/loser affair. Far too many people speak in platitudes, hide behind lofty vision statements, and work to blow the other boat out of the water at all costs. Many people are very adept at using language to simplify very complex situations that actually demand a higher level of language facility. Dialogue is a way of using language that fits better with team structures and with broader scopes of responsibility. Dialogue is also a set of techniques for developing language facility, and like any skills, these must be defined, explained, demonstrated, and practiced.

Materials

None.

Approximate Time Required

20–60 minutes.

49

Through the Looking Glass

Objective

To rate yourself according to the perception you have of how others see you.

Procedure

Develop a self-assessment tally form similar to the example below. Give one to each team member. At a team meeting, ask each team member to indicate with a Y (Yes) or N (No) his or her perception of how each other person in the team sees him or her. This exercise is essentially a readout on feedback. The finished exercise should be a page full of Ys and Ns.

Put names of team members, including your own, across the top of the form. Include a rating of how you perceive yourself. Put characteristics of good team members down the side of the form. Get several team members to help you design the form, especially the choice of good characteristics. (See page 148.)

Ask team members to simply reflect upon the patterns in their tally, and resolve to themselves to make any adjustments needed. Do the exercise in silence.

Repeat the exercise periodically throughout the year, comparing results and analyzing perception patterns.

Discussion Questions

None. This is an exercise to be done in silence, as part of instituting work practices that encourage reflection before action. If questions are asked, answer them but tell the team that this exercise is a self-reflection exercise. Action should follow it at a later time.

Notes

Y? or N?

	Self	Tom	Penny	Chris	Linda	Astrid
1. helpful						
2. believable						
3. committed						
4. honest						
5. expert						
6. understanding						
7. sensitive						
8. productive						
9. quality						
10. flexible						

A way to expand this exercise is to use a rating scale of 1, 2, 3, or 4 to indicate a range of responses. Or, any particularly troubling trait could be more deeply analyzed using a scale of any kind;1 to 4 is my favorite because it avoids a center point and generally on opinion data yields enough information to generate an action response. 1 to 7 or 1 to 10 are also popular scales because they structure more specific responses.

Materials

A self-assessment trait team member form, to be created by a subteam with facilitator guidance; a copy for each team member.

Approximate Time Required

5–10 minutes.

50

Left-Hand Column

Objective

To construct a "Left-Hand Column" exercise of self-assessment regarding assumptions and other thinking and language that impede communication.

Procedure

This is another kind of self-assessment. This one should be done first in silence, then in discussion with the rest of the team at a team meeting or training session. It is an exercise that brings hidden assumptions to the surface and helps team members to become more aware of their thinking patterns and how their language can distort reality.

Fold a piece of paper vertically so that there's a left-hand column and a right-hand column. On this paper, team members will write a script, actually two scripts, of a recent conversation with someone at work that either led nowhere or was outright counterproductive. Such conversations are often held over some problem or thorny issue. Use as many pieces of paper, thus folded, as you need for the full script.

Instruct team members to write in the right-hand column first. In this column, reconstruct the conversation as it was said, using your name and the other person's name as if you were writing a play. Include everything—anger, guilt, annoyance, resentment, outbursts, hidden agendas, etc. When you've finished the right-hand column recording the way the conversation went, unfold the paper so that the blank Left-Hand Column is before you. In it, now write what you were actually thinking and feeling as each of the "scripted" words were said. In essence, write the true script of the conversation.

After the writing has been completed, debrief the exercise by analysis of the scripts. Indicate what positive results could be expected if the Left-Hand Column script had been the script in use. This kind of chart on a whiteboard or flip chart can guide the discussion:

Notes

what should be (LEFT HAND)	what is (RIGHT HAND)	results

An example might be:

(LH) face the problem ... (RH) just keep smiling ... resolution by Friday

(LH) follow the model ... (RH) forget the model ... consistency, trust

Discussion Questions

During discussion after the script writing, ask team members to share with the team some of the most obvious contrasts in their scripts. Keep the focus on analysis of differences between the expressed thinking and the true thinking. Ask the team to construct a list of the miserable, unproductive, and even destructive behaviors they have been perpetuating. Ask them then to construct a set of guidelines for more authentic behaviors and what the expected results might be. Keep the team talking as long as the discussion is productive.

This is an exercise devised by Harvard University professor Chris Argyris, and popularized by Peter Senge and consultants at Innovation Associates, Framingham, MA. There are many take-offs on this that often show up at workshops. All have the characteristic "what is" and "what should be" aspects that encourage the participant to discover a more authentic approach to work.

Materials

Several pieces of paper folded in half vertically per team member; pencils; flip chart or whiteboard and markers.

Approximate Time Required

1–1½ hours.

51

Upside and Downside

Objective

To identify the Upside (good effects) and Downside (bad effects) of mental habits that support team learning.

Procedure

This is an exercise in identification and sorting out. It requires careful and precise analysis of what might seem to be "motherhood and apple pie" behaviors—behaviors that seem so natural and ideal that people often think of them in a fuzzy sort of undifferentiated way. It is an exercise in clear thinking.

Five of these behaviors will be analyzed by the team working as a group, in brainstorming fashion. That is, all related ideas are welcome; there's no right or wrong. Using two flip charts side by side so that both can be seen at once by participants is the easiest way to facilitate the exercise.

On one flip chart, write the 5 behaviors or habits of mind that support team learning. These are:

1. Taking prudent risks.

2. Continuously assessing one's own successes and failures in the context of the work of the team.

3. Actively and intentionally seeking others' ideas.

4. Listening.

5. Problem solving with an open mind.

On the other flip chart, make an Upside ... Downside chart, keyed to each of the 5 behaviors. It should look something like this:

Notes

	UPSIDE	DOWNSIDE

1. **risk**

2. **self-assessment**

3. **seek ideas**

4. **listening**

5. **open mind**

Be sure to allow enough space in each category of behavior for several responses under both Upside and Downside. Open the discussion and record responses. Encourage brainstorming.

Discussion Questions

It's no secret that teamwork requires a good dose of humility as well as a forthright assertiveness on the part of each team member. These are not habits of mind or behavior that typically have characterized our workplaces. Like all habits, new habits of mind and body must be identified, valued, promoted, and practiced in order for change to occur.

During this exercise, simply ask team members to think about both the upsides and the downsides of behaving in each new way, and systematically fill in the chart. Facilitate an open discussion. If they have trouble getting started, suggest that risking taking, for example, has the upside of the exhilaration of being outside of one's normal comfort zone, that is, the thrill of "stretch"; risk taking has a downside of possibly producing failure, embarrassment, or lost time.

In a recent book on leadership, Harvard University's John Kotter defines similar habits of the lifelong learner who would be a leader. The five habits suggested in this exercise are adapted for a team setting from his work. See J.P. Kotter, *Leading Change*, Boston: Harvard Business School Press, 1996, chapter 12, "Leadership and Lifelong Learning."

Materials

Two flip charts and markers.

Approximate Time Required

20–30 minutes.

52

White Space

Objective

To use the analogy of the graphics term, "white space," as a stimulus to finding previously hidden opportunities for business growth; to experience the learning technique of "seeing something that isn't there," as one tool in future planning.

Procedure

This is a focusing exercise, appropriate for the first few minutes of a team meeting that deals with strategy development. Facilitate an exploratory discussion of the whole team, using a whiteboard or flip chart to write down responses for later reference.

Explain what white space is, for those who have not encountered the term before. It is a graphics term that refers to the blank spaces around words, numbers, and graphic designs on a page or screen. White space is not empty space; to a layout artist or graphics designer it is a critical and often carefully designed space meant to enhance or illuminate the other elements on the page. In that sense, it is full of potential, not empty, and it is very meaningful to the whole. Often, in fact, white space provides the drama and motivation for the learning that follows.

Using the conceptual basis of white space, team members identify, define, and discuss organizational and market white spaces that will affect their company's and their team's future work. Start them off with some cues; make a short list of items such as:

- where to find leverage for more resources (the resources white space)

- economic threats on the horizon (the economy white space)

- what customers will probably need soon (the customer need white space)

- changes in the company's structure (the organization chart white space)

Ask the team to think of more areas in which white space can be discovered, and add them to your list. Then identify, define, and discuss the specific fea-

Notes

tures of those white spaces. Take the results of this exercise forward into a strategy planning session.

Discussion Questions

Continue to remind the team to search for relationships between the core competencies or basic strengths of the company and these white space areas. Use this exercise to validate the company's (team's) mission and values. During discussion, focus back on core competencies whenever you can.

Professors and consultants Gary Hamel and C.K. Prahalad wrote extensively about strategizing in their best-selling book, *Competing for the Future,* Boston: Harvard Business School Press, 1994. One of the companies featured in the book is Electronic Data Systems, EDS, Dallas, TX. Its efforts at training waves of managers in futuring techniques are reported in particularly interesting fashion on pages 114ff. People don't naturally think creatively when they plan and strategize. EDS learned how to do this; others can learn it too. Understanding white space is a small step in the right direction.

Materials

Flip chart or whiteboard and markers.

Approximate Time Required

15–30 minutes.

53

I Own This Business

Objective

To develop criteria for performance measurements for the team.

Procedure

This is a team exercise structured to stretch the thinking of individual team members about team management issues. It is particularly for the team that wants to be self-managed. Facilitate the exercise at two flip charts that all can see.

This exercise is in three parts, one following the other. The first task is for the team as a whole to figure out what the categories of team performance are and list them down the side of the flip chart page. The second task is get a show of hands from the team regarding who believes that he or she has responsibility in each category. The third task is to develop specific measures and timelines for each category.

The flip chart for tasks one and two should be a matrix with the names of team members across the top, and numbers 1 through 15 down the left side, next to which the categories of team performance will be listed. Next to this flip chart should be another on which to record the actual development of specific measures for each category (see page 156). By the end of the session, all team members should feel the weight of responsibility of self-management, but they should also feel confident that an equitable performance measurement system is in place.

Begin the exercise by suggesting that each team member say this to himself or herself, and then decide what the categories of performance really are:

> **"I own this business; therefore I must be accountable for _____
> _____."**

Repeat this statement periodically as the team is deciding what categories to list. Drive home the point that self-man-

Notes

EJN SJM KND RCD		MEASURES	
1.		1. o	(p. 1 of 5)
2.		o	
3.		o	
4.		o	
5.		2. o	
6.		o	
7.		o	
.		o	
.		3. o	
14.		o	
15.		o	

aging teams are truly accountable for the ways in which they do business and for results. These are some categories that teams sometimes miss; give them cues if they're having trouble thinking in management terms:

lead time   throughput   information management
housekeeping   developing leadership   recruiting

Discussion Questions

The exercise can get tricky when you ask for a show of hands regarding each person's responsibility in each category. Record a check mark in the appropriate person's column for each hand raised. Get group consensus about any who feel that they are not responsible for that particular category—you'll discover pretty fast where your leadership is and where it needs to be developed. You'll also see by this part of the exercise how subteams might function within the larger team. This can be an exercise in understanding.

One of the biggest challenges in self-managed teams is to be realistic about the capabilities, desires, and goals of individuals regarding management of the team. There are a great many "nice words" about teamwork, but until the team goes through a learning exercise like this one, dealing with the details of personal responsibility and measurement, those nice words remain just that—words. Accountability must have an element of "stretch" in it; goals must be attainable and reasonable, and, of course, within the power of the team as it exists and the resources available in order to accomplish those goals.

Materials

Two flip charts and markers.

Approximate Time Required

1 hour.

54

80/20 and 50/5

Objective

To use Pareto's Law as a conceptual model to prioritize team activities.

Procedure

This exercise is the initial part of a planning process. In it, team members will rank order a list of activities for the coming planning period (e.g., 3 months) and assign implementation responsibilities according to Pareto's 80/20 law.

Pareto's Law is often referred to as "the significant few versus the trivial many." It says that when a list of items is arranged in rank order, that is, in *descending order of importance,* the first 20 percent of items generally represent 80 percent of the total value of all items. A corollary to this is that, in addition, the final 50 percent of items generally represent only 5 percent of the total value.

Applying the concept of Pareto's Law to the work of teams is a valuable exercise because it helps team members to focus on doing the tasks and team activities that can be expected to yield the most value to the company. Too often, in their zeal to do everything right, and now that they've been given the authority and freedom to be self-managed, team members try to devote equal energy and resources to all tasks and activities. The 80/20 and 50/5 law discovered by French economist Vilfredo Pareto is a helpful guide when developing a team action plan.

Using a flip chart that all can see, facilitate development of a list of at least 20 top-priority team activities for the next period (1 month, 3 months, etc.) Try for 40 items if possible. Rank order the activities in descending order of importance.

If you are having trouble deciding, use a rating scale of 1 to 10, have each team member vote on each activity, and use the tally of numbers as a way of making a decision. If you have 20 items, expect the first 4 items to represent 80 percent of the total value to the organization; if you have 40 items, expect the first 8 items to represent 80 percent of the total value. The more items, the better the statistics will work.

Use Pareto's Law as a guideline for assigning resources to activities, recognizing that more investment (of people, time, or money) at the top of the list might be the wisest approach to action. It's very tempting to make the list and assign jobs so that everybody gets at least one item to do; resist this tendency, and pay attention to Pareto's Law instead.

Discussion Questions

Keep asking, "What are the most important activities for this team?" Important can mean: capable of generating the most profit, producing the most cash flow, engendering the most trust, helping the most people, yielding the highest quality, or whatever else you can define as important. Eventually, ask the team to agree on the top 20 percent of important activities and on their rank order.

In teamwork especially, it is important that everyone is working on the right issues and not working on projects and activities that have little payoff. 80/20 and 50/5 can help teams do the right thing!

Materials

Flip chart and markers.

Approximate Time Required

60–90 minutes.

55

Diamonds Are a Team's Best Friend

Objective

To focus on the decision point (diamond) in a flowchart of a team process and to practice using decision points as part of in-process evaluation.

Procedure

Review the basic forms used in flowcharting a work process: ovals, rectangles, and diamonds—*ovals* for the start or the input, and the finish or the output; *rectangles* for the subprocesses, and *diamonds* for decision points during the development of the process. Draw a short sample flowchart on a whiteboard (that can be erased easily) to illustrate the features of flowcharting.

Now ask the team to construct a flowchart, concentrating first on the rectangles, naming in order the subprocesses or activities that need to occur. Have the team itself draw the rectangles—anyone who wants to can come forward to add a rectangle. Be sure that they leave space between rectangles, so that diamonds can be indicated without too much erasure. As a working example, choose either an office routine like making coffee or producing a team newsletter, or a job-related activity like conducting a training needs assessment or hiring a training consultant. Let this be a team activity; facilitate the team's deciding the proper sequence for the rectangles.

When all have agreed that these are the subprocesses needed, ask them to focus on where the decision points (diamonds) will come. Tell the team that "Diamonds Are a Team's Best Friend," and shift the focus to the points in the process where a decision diamond should be inserted. Ask the team to insert diamonds, naming the decision and classifying each decision as to whether it is a cyclical kind of decision that must be repeated many times, or a complete re-do of the process. Ask the team to identify approximately how long the branching processes might take, and how much time and expense they might add to the process as a whole. Focus on

Notes

the idea that between initial input and final output of any process, there are decision points—inspection points—where important considerations and potential changes in direction occur. These inspection points are internal to the process, and are thus known as in-process inspection. They are the hallmarks of continuous improvement to and continuous learning about the process. Diamonds are a team's best friend when it comes to process quality. In-process inspection gets rid of problems, even little problems, before they get into the hands of customers and those at the "finish oval."

Discussion Questions

Add a deeper dimension to the discussion of flowchart diamonds by suggesting the creation of an "inspection checklist" at every decision point. Each checklist should answer questions of quantity, percent, or other measurable standard.

> Many good books on in-process evaluation are available from the ASQC Quality Press, Milwaukee, WI, 800-248-1946. One that is especially relevant to flowcharting is Dianne Galloway's *Mapping Work Processes,* published in 1994. She has a particularly good chapter on inspection points and inspection checklists.

Materials

Whiteboard and markers.

Approximate Time Required

20–45 minutes.

56

It's a Numbers Game

Objective

To practice quick thinking about measurement of team success.

Procedure

Divide the team in half and have them line up one behind the other in two subteams. The object of the game is to see which subteam wins the race to specify in quantitative terms what the numerical standards are for the work of the team. Subteams will work in close proximity to each other and write their responses on a whiteboard so that each can see the other's work.

The essence of the game is for each person to write down one standard that can be measured in numbers, and as soon as that person's response has been written, he or she returns to the back of the line, *handing the marker to the next in line,* and the next person takes a turn as quickly as possible, as in a relay race. No two responses from within the subteam should be the same. Subteams may caucus if individuals near the end of the line are having trouble thinking of something that hasn't already been written. The first team finished is declared the winner. Give each member on the winning subteam an **"I'm #1"** blue ribbon (pattern on page 163).

Read all responses from both subteams and verify with the team that all responses are standards that can be measured with numbers. If this is so, continue the play by switching teams. That is, subteam A will now line up in front of subteam B's responses, and vice versa. The task now is for each subteam to assign the specific number measures to each standard—of the other subteam's responses. The game continues in similar "relay" fashion, and the first subteam that completes the task is declared the winner. Give each member on the winning subteam an **"I'm #1"** blue ribbon (pattern on page 163).

Notes

These are examples of a first response, and a second response:

1st. better margins   2nd. from 12% to 13.5%
1st. quicker delivery   2nd. within 3 business days

1st response = standards;
2nd response = a number with which to measure work toward meeting the
                     standard.

Discussion Questions

Facilitate an open discussion of all responses, focusing on the numbers as-signed to each response. Get consensus if you can, modifying any re-sponse with the agreement of team members. Talk about "stretch" targets and where they can be most effective in making work interesting, chal-lenging, and full of learning potential.

> Performance measurement of teams must be done just as performance measurement of individuals must be done. The first step is understanding the importance of numbers, realistic and attainable goals, given who the players are and what the resources are. This game format can help focus team members' attention fully on the narrow tasks of defining measur-able standards; the play adds a heightened sense of clear expression.

Materials

Whiteboard and markers; blue ribbons for team members (equivalent of 1 per person).

Approximate Time Required

1 hour.

It's a Numbers Game

57

360 Degrees Online

Objective

To learn to use the tools for designing a 360-Degree Evaluation online by following some simple rules.

Procedure and Discussion

Before beginning this exercise, team members need some background information on this process of evaluation. A popular and widely used evaluation tool for individual performance is known as "360-Degree Evaluation," by which is meant evaluation by multiple persons who generally have different "angles" on the person being rated. In measurement lingo, this is known as multi-rater assessment, and the goal is to achieve inter-rater reliability because of the design of the instrument and the number and choice of raters.

It has been in use widely for about a decade, and has proven itself a useful employee empowerment tool as well as an effective and accurate performance evaluation methodology. Drawbacks documented in early adoption of the 360-Degree Evaluation model included an unclear role for the supervisor and the exponential amount of time expended on evaluation as the number of raters per evaluatee was increased in order to broaden the rater base.

The 360-Degree Evaluation model seems right for team-based evaluation. However, its implementation can be a costly time-consumer if some safeguards are not designed into the process. The rules that follow can help your team get started in the right direction toward an effective performance evaluation without using up too much time.

1. The person being rated chooses the raters.

2. Six raters generally yield valid and reliable results.

3. Choose an equal number of raters who are peers and who are direct reports. (Suppliers, customers, and staff are also possibilities.)

Notes

4. Allow the supervisor to add to but not delete from the choices of raters.

5. Put the time-consuming processes online: input, administration, scoring, score interpretation, and feedback.

6. Record all time spent online, including each rater's time responding, administration time, accessing feedback, etc. Design the documentation so that it is easy to analyze it, to see trends, and to make efficiency adjustments if necessary.

7. Create clear instructions.

8. In designing the survey, use short sentences or a phrase format in order to minimize reading time.

9. Design according to the "necessary and sufficient" rule: include only criteria that are necessary but all that are sufficient for valid assessment.

10. Allow a one-week period in which raters must complete the survey. Score all responses and provide feedback within the next week. Keep the process confined to a two-week period from input to output.

11. Train everyone involved in advance about how to do the evaluating. Use a classroom training format, present information and instructions to all equally, and give all persons ample opportunity to get their questions answered.

12. In advance and with input from the person being rated, prepare and distribute to all raters a list of job responsibilities/activities, competencies, and performance targets for the person being rated. Prepare this in such a way that it can be visible on the rating survey online, either as an appendix or as the first screen a rater sees when doing the rating.

13. Remember that the only important test of a good evaluation is whether it is useful. Plan ahead for how you intend to use the results; communicate this ahead of time to all raters and persons being rated.

Give team members practice in working with these 13 rules. Make a copy of the 13 rules (page 167) for each person. Review them together, encouraging the team members to make personal notes after each rule as if they were designing their own 360-Degree Evaluation. At some point they will be designing their own; this exercise will give them a head start.

> A good book on the subject is *360-Degree Feedback* by Mark R. Edwards and Ann J. Ewen, NY: AMACOM, 1996.

Materials

Copies of 13 Rules for 360-Degree Evaluation for each person.

Approximate Time Required

20 minutes for this exercise.

13 Rules for 360-Degree Evaluation

personal notes

1. The person being rated chooses the raters.

2. Six raters generally yield valid and reliable results.

3. Choose an equal number of raters who are peers and who are direct reports. (Suppliers, customers, and staff are also possibilities.)

4. Allow the supervisor to add to but not delete from the choices of raters.

5. Put the time-consuming processes online: input, administration, scoring, score interpretation, and feedback.

6. Record all time spent online, including each rater's time responding, administration time, accessing feedback, etc. Design the documentation so that it is easy to analyze it, to see trends, and to make efficiency adjustments if necessary.

7. Create clear instructions.

8. In designing the survey, use short sentences or a phrase format in order to minimize reading time.

9. Design according to the "necessary and sufficient" rule: include only criteria that are necessary but all that are sufficient for valid assessment.

10. Allow a one-week period in which raters must complete the survey. Score all responses and provide feedback within the next week. Keep the process confined to a two-week period from input to output.

11. Train everyone involved in advance about how to do the evaluating. Use a classroom training format, present information and instructions to all equally, and give all persons ample opportunity to get their questions answered.

12. In advance and with input from the person being rated, prepare and distribute to all raters a list of job responsibilities/activities, competencies, and performance targets for the person being rated. Prepare this in such a way that it can be visible on the rating survey online, either as an appendix or as the first screen a rater sees when doing the rating.

13. Remember that the only important test of a good evaluation is whether it is useful. Plan ahead for how you intend to use the results; communicate this ahead of time to all raters and persons being rated.

58

Snow Whites and Grumpies

Objective

To borrow a technique used at Disney for testing the test in 360-Degree Evaluation; ultimately to use a two-test variation of the model in order to determine consistency and validity of results.

Procedure

It's easy to criticize the self-choice feature of 360-Degree Evaluation. This seems particularly problematic in teams, where close and personal relationships are often formed. Observers wonder whether "friends" can truly evaluate "friends." Folks at Disney decided to find out, and so constructed a test evaluation, that is, a testing of the testing process itself.

To do this they did the 360-Degree Evaluation using two rater groups, one they called the Snow Whites (known friends of the evaluatee), and the other they called Grumpies (known non-friends of the evaluatee). What they discovered was that all people take the role of evaluator of another person very seriously, and, in fact, all persons, Snow Whites and Grumpies alike, evaluated in nearly the same way. Friendship did not get in the way; results from the two rater groups were very similar.

When you begin the process of designing your team's 360-Degree Evaluation, consider the Disney experiment. If you must respond to criticism of the "friendship factor," use a two-group test in order to validate results. Remain true to the evaluatee choice feature of the process, however; ask each team member to list six of his or her own "Snow Whites" and six "Grumpies."

Discussion Questions

When choosing both Snow Whites and Grumpies, it may be helpful to guide the selection process by asking some of the following questions:

- Are these raters equally familiar with users' perspectives?

Notes

- Are these raters equally committed to the work of this team?

- Do both sets of raters understand participative work challenges and rewards?

- Do both sets of raters demonstrate in their own jobs a responsible and accountable position?

- Are both sets of raters adequate communicators? (Do they listen, give and receive feedback, use words to the advantage of others, not only themselves, etc.?)

Discuss with the team that these questions have nothing to do with friendship or nonfriendship; they focus on characteristics that transcend personal relationships, but make for good evaluators. Choosing raters is an important task; these considerations can help.

Before embarking on the doubly time-consuming process of using a two-rater-group approach, consider the downside, which, of course, is that twice as many people and time resources are expended in the evaluation. It may, however, be the only way to avoid criticism of the process and to gain acceptance of the findings.

Materials

Pencils and paper.

Approximate Time Required

A few minutes to construct a list of Snow Whites and Grumpies.

59

Treasure Hunt

Objective

To find (identify the location of) the best sources of data upon which to construct team evaluation.

Procedure

Play this as a "mental" treasure hunt game. Use "gold coins" (pattern on page 173) and a "treasure chest" to help set the context for a treasure hunt.

Set aside about a 30-minute time period at a regular team meeting, during which time all team members are asked to figure out where in the company and its stakeholders (suppliers, customers, board, neighbors, shareholders, competitors, etc.) the best data exist upon which the evaluation should be based. Encourage expansive thinking. Continue on with the regular business of the meeting, encouraging team members to "parallel process," that is, since the timer is clicking within the 30 minutes, team members will have to think of where to find the treasures at the same time they are participating in the regular business of the meeting.

Distribute about 20 gold coins (on gold copy paper) to each team member at the beginning of the meeting. Ask team members to put their names on one side of each coin. The other side is reserved for the identification of the "treasure," that is, the source of the data. As each team member thinks of one or more treasures, he or she brings the coin(s) to a treasure box (old jewelry box, candy box, or cigar box) at the front of the room. This identification process continues until the 30 minutes is up.

At the end of the 30 minutes, the meeting agenda should be so planned that it leads into evaluation design. To begin, the leader/trainer shakes up the treasure and reads the gold coins one by one as the entire team votes on the quality of that particular source of data. Use a 1, 2, 3 or a 1, 2, 3, 4 scale. Ask "How many give it a 1 (low)? A 2 (medi-

Notes

um)? A 3 (high)?" Record responses on a flip chart or whiteboard in a column of team members' names. Reward the person with the highest score—the most treasure—with a gold nugget paperweight, a bag of gold coin chocolates, or some other treasure-related trinket.

Discussion Questions

This is an exercise in putting up one's mental antennae, and in parallel processing. It is an analog of good team thinking, since that also requires alert antennae and parallel processing. During the regular business of the meeting, stop occasionally to encourage treasure hunting; remind folks that they are being expected to do two things at once.

Get a team member to help you read the coins as you do the weighting of items and the recording of votes. Expect items such as: quality reports, calendars, journals and time logs, absentee reports, safety reports, audit reports, sales, deliveries, inventory, customer complaints, etc. Use these items as cues if people have a hard time getting started. Urge them to be more creative than this, and to look harder for the really good treasure.

When you read the coins to the group, be sure to read the name of the person as well as that person's suggested source, i.e., both sides of the coin. You'll get a great sense of what the team thinks is important with this game.

Materials

20 gold coins for each team member (see page 173); whiteboard or flip chart and markers.

Approximate Time Required

30–45 minutes.

Treasure Hunt

Copy this page on gold paper 4 times for each team member; cut out coins.

60

360-Degree Follow-Up

Objective

To observe yourself in a leadership position through an unobtrusive audiotape recording of yourself; to conduct a self-assessment against predetermined standards in order to learn from the results.

Procedure

Plan to tape record yourself in a leadership position such as facilitating a team meeting, training others, or functioning as a mentor. Get agreement from others involved and set up the recorder in an unobtrusive spot. Tell the team that you are doing a self-assessment and appreciate their cooperation. Then forget about the tape recorder and do what you set out to do.

Plan ahead regarding what you expect of yourself as a leader so that you self-assess according to standards set ahead of the taping. For example, you might tie the results of a 360-Degree Evaluation to a taping session, focusing on particular items of feedback that you'd like to work on in order to improve; or you might purposely design a different way of leading than you are used to using in order to see how your design worked. You might have self-evaluation as one of your own personal learning activities for a particular performance period, and want to experiment with various ways of doing self-assessments.

Play back the tape two days later, with a structured self-assessment rating sheet in front of you. Stop the tape at predetermined places, such as every three minutes, in order to take a reading on your behavior, attitudes, competence, and overall performance during the previous segment.

Discussion Questions

There are numerous ways in which to structure the questions you'll ask yourself regarding your own leadership. Here's just one example:

Suppose that you have been a mentor, and your feedback has been that you're a little bit too much of a "controller"

175

Notes

and a "know-it-all." You realize that you often come on too strong, but were always told that that's what made a good leader—being decisive, well informed, and strong. Now that you're in a team, those attitudes and behaviors don't work so well, and you've determined to learn to change. You develop a self-assessment worksheet something like this:

date _____	situation _____		
	controller	learner	possible corrective action
seg. 1			
seg. 2			
seg. 3			
seg. 4			
etc.			

As you listen to yourself in leadership interaction, you'll place a check mark in the appropriate column and make a quick note regarding possible corrective action if any is needed. You will constantly ask yourself, "Was my attitude and behavior more like my old self, the controller, or more like my new self, the learner?" and, "What can I do to take corrective action?"

> Numerous learning organization thinkers and pioneers in the team movement have said time and again that learning faster than one's competition is probably the only viable long-term, competitive strategy that will work in today's business world. We all need to create ways of learning smarter and better from our work and by ourselves. This kind of process is one that works, but it takes ego strength, commitment to learning, and time.

Materials

Audiotape recorder and tape; self-assessment worksheet/documentation form.

Approximate Time Required

Several hours.

61
Toy Box

Objective

To identify and define mental tools required to shape the skills needed for successful teamwork; to name the "cognitive artifacts" that complement our abilities and strengthen our mental powers.

Procedure

Do this exercise at a team meeting or training session. Use the analogy of filling up a toy box with wonderful toys (cognitive artifacts), old and new "friends" that help to make life richer and more full of meaning. Draw a picture of a big open toy box on a whiteboard or flip chart for team members to see. Around this drawing, facilitate a discussion about the "toys" we'd like to put in our box. Use this exercise to expand the team's thinking about mental processes and abilities, and about how to use these "toys" to enhance work.

Ask team members to call out their favorite "toys." When they have identified a cognitive artifact, make a symbol of it, give it a name, and draw it into the toy box. Collect a dozen or so cognitive artifacts in similar fashion from any team member who has one to suggest. Fill the toy box; then facilitate a discussion of the composite that's in the toy box and what that picture of "toys" says about the team.

Discussion Questions

Cognitive artifacts, according to cognitive scientists, are physical and mental tools that help us **remember better, think better,** and **reason better.** They assist our brains in expanding our intelligence and thinking more creatively. Human beings are good at creating cognitive artifacts; it is generally agreed that a person plus an artifact is more powerful than either alone, and that it is good to be aware of what kinds of cognitive artifacts we have created and of the ways in which we use them.

These are some examples: *mental tools* such as reading, arithmetic, language, logic, filing systems, sketching, listing,

Notes

outlining; and *physical tools* such as whiteboards, markers, pencils, calculators, computers, erasers, tapes, disks. Thousands of categories and subcategories can be named.

The question to ask of team members is:

"What cognitive artifacts ('toys') do you use to stimulate and enhance your intellectual capacity?"

Or,

"You plus what 'toys' will increase the effect of your personal and team performance?"

The point is for team members to learn to search beneath the surface of their habitual work patterns to find places to foster growth. Learning involves the tough work of discovery and painstaking self-analysis.

One of today's best-loved cognitive psychologists is Donald Norman, founding Chair of the Department of Cognitive Sciences at University of California, San Diego, and currently a Fellow at Apple Computer Inc. Norman's book, *Things That Make Us Smart,* Reading, MA: Addison-Wesley, 1993, gives a complete overview of cognitive artifacts, and puts forth the point of view that our real task in creating and using cognitive artifacts is to make the environment and the tasks of living and working fit the person, and not the other way around. He staunchly defends human attributes in the age of technology, and cautions against allowing ourselves to be enticed or simply entertained by technology. Knowing a little bit more about cognitive artifacts can help us be more intentional and effective learners, and better stewards of what truly makes us human.

Materials

Whiteboard and markers.

Approximate Time Required

15–30 minutes.

62
Discovering Digital Literacy

Objective

To help team members discover the characteristics of digital literacy by differentiating them and contrasting them from the more familiar kind of literacy.

Procedure

This is an unscrambling game, to be played individually by each team member. It's the sort of pencil and paper game you might typically find in a kids' activity book. Use this game to lead into a serious discussion of how thinking should change in order to maximize the advantages of the Internet and World Wide Web, and how language must be preserved, defended, changed, and used to both enhance working on the Net and guard against abuses of working on the Net.

Distribute to each team member a copy of the unscrambling game found on page 181. Ask them to unscramble the terms, writing each term in the appropriate column, "New Literacy" or "Old Literacy." Add any other pairs of terms you can think of.

When all have completed the game, ask them to exchange papers with a partner and agree among themselves as to what the correct sorting is. If there seems to be disagreement, facilitate an understanding of other points of view and definitions, or check the listings against this "correct" listing below:

New Literacy	Old Literacy
build content	present content
interactive	passive
customized/ customizable	content-limited
immediacy of correspondents	separation of correspondents
willingness to share	embarrassment, self-con- sciousness
multitasking	serial
distribution transparency	distribution obstacles
ephemeral words	fixed words
diverse	programmed
invites in	broadcasts out

Discussion Questions

Ask for someone to read his or her list of "New Literacy" descriptors and to initiate a discussion about what each descriptor means. Ask for examples from team members' own online experience as each characteristic is discussed. Keep discussion expanding, in discovery mode.

> This is a "discovery exercise," a process that is modeled by the gimmick of the game itself. That is, the analysis, sorting, and choosing are all related discovery processes. Seeing the whole, then its parts, helps the learner to more carefully differentiate. The "New" list and the "Old" list further help to reinforce comparison, thereby clarifying the new. Discovery is an important team learning tool. Sometimes people have to simply take the time to practice it in order to remember how it's done.

Materials

A Discovering Digital Literacy unscrambling game for each team member (page 181).

Approximate Time Required

15–20 minutes.

Discovering Digital Literacy

Unscrambling Game

build content

embarrassment, self-consciousness

present content

willingness to share

customized/customizable

separation of correspondents

content-limited

immediacy of correspondents

multitasking

interactive

serial

ephemeral words

passive

distribution transparency

fixed words

diverse

distribution obstacles

programmed

invites in

broadcasts out

Rewrite each term above in the appropriate column below:

New Literacy	**Old Literacy**
•	•
•	•
•	•
•	•
•	•
•	•
•	•
•	•
•	•
•	•
•	•
•	•
•	•
•	•
•	•
•	•
•	•
•	•

63
Daily Walk on the Web

Objective

To begin to develop a personal information strategy using the tool of "journal" analysis.

Procedure

This exercise is akin to writing a journal; it is also akin to storytelling. However, it is not quite either. The purpose of the exercise is to say aloud, to recount experiences of, one's own journey on the Internet/World Wide Web on a typical day; and from that, with the help of the team, to construct the beginnings of a personal information strategy.

At a team meeting or training session, ask each team member in turn to recount a typical experience of "walking on the Web." Ask that the narratives be chronological, that is, first I did this, then this, and then this. Ask that the narratives be expanded into stories of what happened, where the thinking or playing went, which information was accessed, discarded, or used, and how or why.

Discussion Questions

At the end of each "Daily Walk on the Web," facilitate a discussion of the team about one's own personal relationship to information and to the process of learning online. Suggest that learning styles can be expected to vary, that content choices will be evident, that various skill levels for online knowledge acquisition will be demonstrated, and that individual differences in ability to understand and ability to make use of data will be highlighted.

The point is that online learning, like any learning, is a highly individualized matter and demands competency development of various sorts for different individuals. The old admonition to "Know thyself" is as critical in online learning as it is in any other learning context.

Notes

Those who think about how to maximize the power of learners online generally agree that the key or core competency of the Internet user is the ability to be a critical thinker, that is, to exhibit strong evaluation, synthesis, and analysis skills, and to be able to suspend judgment within time for reflection. The skills of "smelling a rat" and "crap detection" are also important online learning competencies. Walking tall on the Web is about mastering concepts, approaches to information, and ideas. Team learners need to think about how they want to take that walk, and to be able to articulate and practice their own learning strategies in systematic, intentional ways.

Materials

None.

Approximate Time Required

20–40 minutes.

	Game	Page

Needs Analysis

64. Temperature Readout 187
65. Peanut Butter Sandwich 191
66. Step Right Up 193
68. Biology 101 201
69. Knights of the Round Table . . . 203
70. Shop 'Til You Drop 205
71. Disconnect the Dots 207
72. PTS Syndrome 209
81. Clouds 231
83. A Better Game 235
88. Oracle 249
89. Vices of the Virtual 253
91. Tell Me a Different Story 259
94. If You Were CIO 265
95. Personal Trainer 267
97. Behind the Scenes 273

Improving Communication

72. PTS Syndrome 209
74. Disturbing the Peace 213
75. City on a Hill 215
76. "I Have a Dream" 217
84. Mindmapping 237
86. Open Up 245
87. Castle 247
89. Vices of the Virtual 253
90. Hypertext Hurdles 255
95. Personal Trainer 267
96. Triple Self-Portrait 269

Evaluation

67. Light and Shadow 197
81. Clouds 231
89. Vices of the Virtual 253
90. Hypertext Hurdles 255
95. Personal Trainer 267

Roles and Expectations

69. Knights of the Round Table . . . 203
73. Job Modeling 211
75. City on a Hill 215
76. "I Have a Dream" 217
79. Fashion Show 223
80. Expert System 227
82. Play Ball! 233
84. Mindmapping 237
85. Friendly Robots 241

SECTION THREE
Unleashing Creativity

Games Listed by Team Training Topic

Game   *Page*

Roles and Expectations *(continued)*

87. Castle *247*
95. Personal Trainer *267*
98. Fishtank *275*

Individualism within Teams

67. Light and Shadow *197*
72. PTS Syndrome *209*
73. Job Modeling *211*
80. Expert System *227*
84. Mindmapping *237*
87. Castle *247*
88. Oracle *249*
93. Past Is Prologue *263*
94. If You Were CIO *265*
95. Personal Trainer *267*
96. Triple Self-Portrait *269*
97. Behind the Scenes *273*
100. Tell Me You Love Me *279*

Problem Solving

66. Step Right Up *193*
81. Clouds *231*
83. A Better Game *235*
86. Open Up *245*
99. Interior Decorator *277*

Process Improvement

65. Peanut Butter Sandwich *191*
68. Biology 101 . . . . *201*
70. Shop 'Til You Drop *205*
71. Disconnect the Dots *207*
77. Think-*ing* *219*
78. Crystal Ball *221*
80. Expert System *227*
83. A Better Game *235*
85. Friendly Robots *241*
92. Obstacle Course *261*
95. Personal Trainer *267*
98. Fishtank *275*

Recognition

100. Tell Me You Love Me *279*

Trust

None in this section; see Sections 1 and 2

64
Temperature Readout

Objective

To elicit an emotional readout from team members regarding system design as it affects the team's goals.

Procedure

Hand out a copy of the three thermometers (page 189) to each team member. Their task is to make a mark on each thermometer indicating how they feel each particular kind of system is able to facilitate the team's goals. (For example, if you have 3 goals, you'll have 9 marks on the thermometers.)

At the end of the marking task, go around the room and ask for the temperature readouts. Do this any way you choose—make it a noisy affair in which all call out their numbers at once, or a quiet and orderly feedback one by one around the table, or a systematic collection of data in a frequency count complete with means, medians, and modes.

The point of the exercise and the metaphor is to suggest a sort of set point for organizational health. If you use the human body's temperature of 98.6° as the set point, you could suggest that <u>un</u>health or "disease" could be either below or above that, and team members might want to keep 98.6 as a reference point as they do the exercise.

Discussion Questions

Choose up to three of the team's stated goals and ask them as questions. Sample goals might be: trust? added value? communication? empowerment? best in class? Begin the exercise by asking the team to take the temperature of the organization within its ideal system. Each team member should be taking the temperatures of each *system* as it pertains to each goal. Explain this to the team, then simply ask, "What's the system temperature for _____ (trust)?" "What's the system temperature for _____ (added value)?" and so on.

Notes

Teams are often given the responsibility for making change—real, systemic change, not just procedural change. Sometimes an exercise like this can help folks see the possibilities in various systems. Creative thinking is not easy for many people; people need cues and sparks in order to get into a creative frame of mind. This exercise, with its emotional health undercurrent, can get some creative juices flowing. Follow it up with more divergent thinking about healthy organizations.

Materials

A Temperature Readout handout for each team member (see page 189).

Approximate Time Required

15 minutes.

Temperature Readout

closed system
stability
cohesion
security
control

open system
flexibility
collaboration
consensus
authenticity

random system
individuality
variety/diversity
excitement
unpredictability

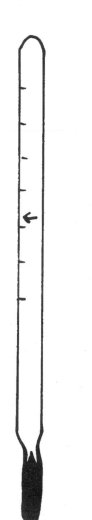

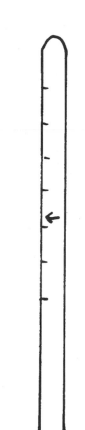

CLOSED

OPEN

RANDOM

65

Peanut Butter Sandwich

Objective

To model the "systems paradigm" by making a peanut butter and jelly sandwich for a teammate.

Procedure

Ahead of time, choose a team member to do this exercise with you in front of the whole team. It is an exercise in clarifying the systems model: inputs, process, outputs, and feedback in service of an ultimate customer. Use the making of a peanut butter and jelly sandwich for a colleague as a metaphor for defining the elements of the systems model.

Begin the exercise a few days ahead of time when you ask your colleague what kind of peanut butter, jelly, and bread he or she prefers. Ask about butter or margarine and any other possible ingredients for the best possible peanut butter and jelly sandwich.

At the team meeting, assemble all ingredients for the peanut butter and jelly sandwich you intend to make. Be sure to bring the tools you'll need, for example, cutting board, paper towels, moistened sponge, a spreader, a knife for cutting the sandwich, a plate on which to serve it, a napkin, etc.

Write on a whiteboard or flip chart for all to see the five elements of the "systems paradigm":

input ... process ... output ... feedback ... customer

The task of the team is to watch you make the sandwich and distinguish in their minds what parts of the activity and the finished product are related to each of the five system elements.

After you serve the sandwich to your colleague, debrief the exercise and get consensus on what the system elements were for the "sandwich game." Be sure to include your customer needs assessment and your customer service.

Notes

Discussion Questions

In new teams especially, it is often hard for folks to differentiate among process and outputs. Go slowly during the construction of the sandwich; involve your "customer" if you like, or choose to have the customer silent until the product is delivered.

Be prepared for surprises—people sometimes really get into this game. The customer might decide that she or he really can't eat a peanut butter and jelly sandwich without a glass of cold milk. How will you handle this? How much is your customer worth? Extend the play for as long as it is instructive. Ask the team what they'd do.

> Stretch your team's thinking to typical team processes, and ask them to do a similar systems analysis of each, differentiating the system features into the five elements of inputs, process, outputs, feedback, and customer. Here are some possibilities: conducting a training class, managing a project, preparing a newsletter, planning a company picnic, approving travel expenses.

Materials

Ingredients for a peanut butter and jelly sandwich.

Approximate Time Required

20–60 minutes.

66

Step Right Up

Objective

To help team members think in terms of levels of emotion by using the image of a set of stairs.

Procedure

Draw a picture of a set of stairs, similar to the one on page 195, on a whiteboard for all to see. You'll need the eraser for this exercise, and you might want to use two different colors of markers.

Do this as a team exercise in which all participate as the spirit moves them. It's a left-brain approach to a right-brain topic, emotional health, or, as Daniel Goleman, best-selling author, says, "emotional intelligence." The exercise involves analyzing and ordering into a hierarchy various levels of emotion. The stairs metaphor may help people to think about the levels more clearly.

Begin the exercise by asking the team to name some major emotions, for example, love, anger, joy, fear, sadness, and surprise. Ask them to identify which one or two have relevance in the workplace. Take two of these as examples for the exercise, one positive one and one negative one, for example, fear and joy. Deal with them one at a time. Ask how these emotions have relevance at this particular workplace.

Write the word "fear" or "joy" on the top step, representing the highest point in the hierarchy. Then ask team members to think of lesser "steps" that need to be taken to get to that top step. Ask them to name the related but less strong emotions and arrange them on the steps in order. An example in the emotion of fear might be "edginess" at the bottom, "misgivings," "dread," "anxiety," and so on. "Joy" might be made up of lesser emotions such as "satisfaction," "amusement," "contentment," "delight," and others. Help the team to see variations in the larger terms. Continue the exercise as long as team members can think of more categories.

Discussion Questions

Very often, teams are admonished to create "joy" in the workplace, or to drive out "fear." Very often, these overarching emotional terms do not mean very much because people don't have an easy way to break them down into more understandable and real emotions that they can do something about. This exercise is designed to facilitate a way of thinking about the grand emotions that typically find their way into team visions and mission statements.

Daniel Goleman, in his 1995 best-seller, *Emotional Intelligence,* NY: Bantam Books, makes the point that emotional intelligence comes before cognitive or intellectual intelligence. He notes that people relate to each other first at an emotional level; "first feelings, then thought" is how he says it.

To be sure, emotions must be recognized and managed at work. Anger turns into violence, fear immobilizes energy, disgust contributes to lack of motivation, and on and on. The first step in managing emotions is to recognize them and understand that they have many steps. It's easier to deal with wariness than to deal with full-blown fear; easier to support folks who have pride in their work than to decree a workplace full of joy.

Materials

Whiteboard, eraser, several colors of markers; pattern of stairs (see page 195) to copy.

Approximate Time Required

10–20 minutes.

Step Right Up

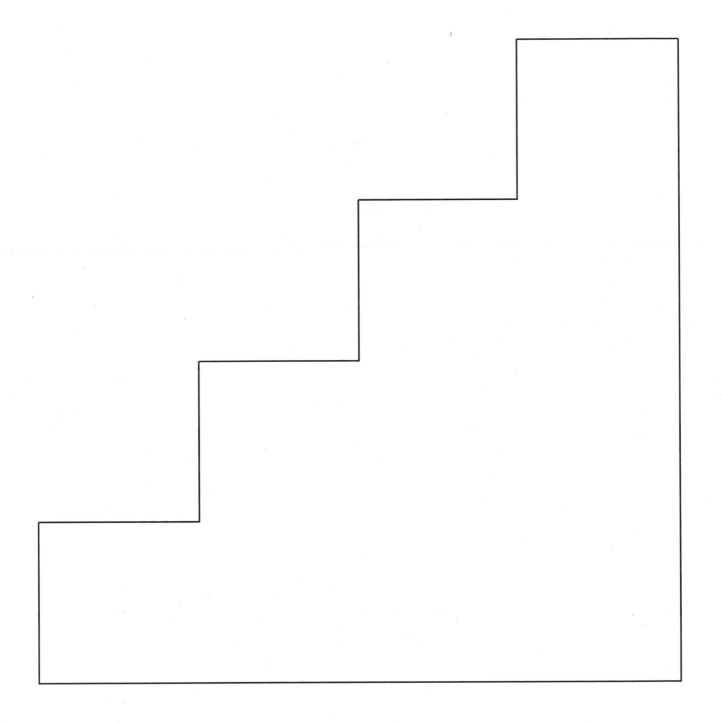

67

Light and Shadow

Objective

To identify one's "light" and "shadow" parts of personality as an exercise in self-awareness.

Procedure

Before a team meeting or training session, make a dozen copies of the yin and yang symbol, page 199. Leave the shadow side as is, but fill in the white side with any one of the "positive" or "obvious" qualities of personality listed here:

balance	dynamism	openness
efficiency	resilience	flexibility
autonomy	orderliness	energy
friendliness	patience	focus
competence	generosity	pride
caring	trust	curiosity

Add any qualities you can think of—qualities that people seem to think are desirable qualities of a team member. Post these yin/yang symbols around the room, each with a different personality quality written on the white side.

Ask team members to look around the room at the symbols, noting that the "shadow" side of each is unnamed. Suggest that they take a few minutes to think of a corresponding "dark" side of each; ask for examples of a few, demonstrating to the entire group how both light and shadow are related.

Then ask team members to choose for themselves 4 of the 12 that seem particularly important from a personal point of view. They should choose qualities of "light" to which they feel particularly related—perhaps those qualities that each person believes are most descriptive of what their personal missions or their own best qualities are. Ask the team to draw their own "light and shadow" symbols on a piece of paper (for themselves only to see), first naming all of the "light" sides. The final task is for each person to name his or her own personal "shadow," that dark side of personality that's hard to deal with, that gets in

Notes

your way, or that light never illuminates. This is an exercise in introspection; team members do not have to share their drawings with each other unless they want to.

Discussion Questions

One way to think about shadows is to think about the opposite of light; another way is to think about the absence of light. Suggest to the team that another way of thinking about the great dichotomies of personality is to think of metaphors of peaks and valleys, sun and moon, dawn and dusk, push and pull, up and down. Suggest to them that life progresses on dynamism, with movement surrounding the whole of life. Challenge their thinking to be honest with themselves, and to first identify what their own shadows are and perhaps why they are there. Only then can action be taken to bring the shadows into the light.

Philosophers, theologians, and counselors, among others, operate in the professional realm of unmasking "whole" personalities in order to help people deal with reality. Management professor and organizational diagnosis expert Margaret Wheatley, in her award-winning 1992/94 book, *Leadership and the New Science* (San Francisco, Berrett-Koehler), describes the process as "independence/interdependence" and talks about the truly marvelous possibilities in "self-renewing systems." Her words are often poetic, and often inspirational. They articulate the challenge for all of us, team members especially, to recognize our complete selves, the dual forces of yin and yang. In Wheatley's words, "The traditional contradictions of order and freedom, change and stasis, being and becoming—these all whirl into a new image that is very ancient—the unifying dance of the great polarities of the universe" (p. 99).

Materials

Pencil and paper for all team members; approximately a dozen yin/yang drawings, marked and ready for posting around the room (see page 199).

Approximate Time Required

40–60 minutes.

Light and Shadow

68

Biology 101

Objective

To expand the team's thinking about organizational diagnosis by analogies with approaches to various fields of study.

Procedure

This is a quick exercise meant to help the team expand their ways of thinking about organizational improvement. Use the fields of physics, biology, and history for starters. Simply introduce a team meeting or training session on organizational diagnosis by suggesting these three analogies:

> **Physics:** discrete objects, inert substances, sequential processes. (Ask the team for more descriptors.)

> **Biology:** related systems, alive substances, parallel processes. (Ask the team for more descriptors.)

> **History:** patterns, development and change, networks of influence. (Ask the team for more descriptors.)

Give cues that encourage people to think expansively. Most folks who have graduated from high school have some familiarity with concepts and thinking requirements for learning in at least these three subjects. Most team members should be able to recognize differences among these three approaches to thinking.

Discussion Questions

After they have begun to diverge in their thinking, suggest that they might now like to refocus on the nature of their own team organization and how it functions and, perhaps, what other ways of thinking might be employed to make the team function better.

Notes

Writer James Bailey has more to say on the subject. Find his home page at http://www.afterthought.com.

Materials

None.

Approximate Time Required

Several minutes.

69

Knights of the Round Table

Objective

To develop a metaphor that enables the examination of assumptions underlying team culture.

Procedure

At a team meeting or training session, sit around a table (that is, not in rows). Say to the team that they should pretend that they are "knights of the round table" whose task it is to create the symbols of their forthcoming crusade. Equate the crusade to changing the corporate culture through their very own team. This exercise is good for a team that has been working together for a while within a larger corporate culture that is still "old style." The elements of both the old style culture and the new style team can help a team to clarify the actual roots of the team and what they might have to do to change them.

Set the stage for a brief acting exercise whereby each person contributes an idea or two as if he or she were a knight about to leave on a crusade. The exercise focuses on identifying the descriptors of the current team culture (good or bad) based on a realistic expectation of where they intend to go on the crusade.

Discussion Questions

Ask your "knights" one by one, *"How will you set off on the crusade?"*

Some typical responses might be: "with two swords and three shields," "with Lovely Lady Luck by my side," "after three days of listening to stories about the faraway place," "with two young knights behind me," "with a gold ring," and so on. As folks get into the play, asides will surface that can lead into a forthright and direct discussion of the nature of the present team culture and where they'd like it to go. You might even get them to name "Lovely Lady Luck" and the "two young knights" if it isn't obvious who these people are.

Unexamined assumptions cause trouble, and often assumptions go un-examined because nobody takes the time to really think creatively about what they are. This exercise stretches the limits of "in the box" thinking.

Materials

None.

Approximate Time Required

5–10 minutes.

70

Shop 'Til You Drop

Objective

To help team members see the value in thinking creatively.

Procedure

Go on a "shopping trip" around your office complex or your factory, looking for evidence of any kind that makes your services or products a better value than your competitors' services or products. Send team members out in pairs, with clipboards, paper, and pencils, to make notes about the "quality merchandise" they discover. Set a time limit, such as two days—"a 2-day sale"—during which the "shopping" must be done. Set a guideline for the number of hours they should spend at this, for example, four hours of actual shopping time. Encourage comparisons with competitors, that is, "comparison shopping." Suggest that team members visit anyone they choose, talk with them, collect information, and write down the features of the company's services and products that add quality and add value. Suggest that they approach this game with the same intensity as they would a "sale" at their favorite store.

Bring these clipboards to a team meeting or training session for discussion of the findings.

Discussion Questions

Ask the team about the process of discovery. To whom did they talk, what was their approach, why did they choose to go there? Then ask for descriptions of the items they found and explanations of how they added value.

Notes

> Experiencing a creative process is hard for many people. So many workplaces stifle creativity in a drive for efficiency and getting the numbers up. This game models a creative process, and is easy enough for people to do. It also can yield some very valuable information about what makes your own company unique. For a good reference on typical team problems (like thinking creatively), see Clay Carr's *Team Leader's Problem Solver,* Englewood Cliffs: Prentice Hall, 1996.

Materials

Clipboards, pencils, and paper.

Approximate Time Required

4 hours spread over 2 days, per team member.

71

Disconnect the Dots

Objective

To figure out how the team's key output (product or service) is interconnected throughout the company; then to figure out the best path to desired change.

Procedure

At a team meeting or training session, use the "play" of a connect the dots game to illustrate some truths about change. The point that you'll eventually make is that change is relatively easy when processes and products, systems and procedures are disconnected from each other. On the other hand, change is extremely difficult when these elements of work are connected (which is the case in most situations). This is an exercise in first seeing the interconnectedness of work elements affecting the team, and then in seeing where change is more likely to succeed in disconnected, or independent, elements. This is an exercise in seeing the difference between interdependence and independence in work processes.

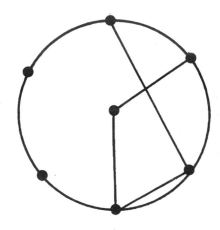

Ask team members to arrange themselves in pairs or triads to work together on the exercise. Ask one member of each subteam to draw a large circle, like the face of a clock, on a piece of paper. Around the perimeter, they'll start by putting large dots at 2, 4, 6, 8, 10, and 12 o'clock positions, so that the paper looks like a circular dot-to-dot game. In the center of the circle, they are to name a primary team product or service and put its dot in the center. The task now is for each subteam to name

Notes

the other dots around the circle, each of which will represent some other thing that the team does or is supposed to do, some process or system that they are implementing. They should work together as a small group and agree on the names of the other dots. The next task is to begin at the center and connect it to any of the other named dots to which it is directly related. Then any of the perimeter dots that are directly related should be connected to each other.

Discussion Questions

The team should quickly see that interconnectedness creates obstacles to quick change, but that change is much easier in any dot that is not connected. Ask questions about how they can facilitate change within the structures they have just described. Also ask if any dots can or should be disconnected in order to succeed at making change.

> An excellent book on the subject of change is Harvard Business School professor John P. Kotter's *Leading Change,* Boston: MA, Harvard Business School Press, 1996. His chapter 9, "Consolidating Gains and Producing More Change," is especially good.

Materials

Pencils and paper.

Approximate Time Required

15 minutes.

72
PTS Syndrome

Objective

*To identify limitations to success in three different categories: **P**ersonal, **T**eam, and **S**upport (PTS); and to dialogue about how to overcome the identified limitations.*

Procedure

Use this game at a meeting at which goals, missions, objectives, or specific project targets are discussed. To play, give each team member a stack of 3×3-inch self-stick notes. Each person must use at least three notes to form one set of PTS responses. All should be encouraged to create more sets, as long as time allows.

One set of PTS includes one self-stick note for the letter P, which stands for Personal limitations to success; one for the letter T, which stands for Team limitations to success; and one for the letter S, which stands for Support limitations to success. Ask each team member to make up one set of notes, P, T, and S, and on each note, write one limitation to success in each category. For example, a "P" limitation might be "I'm shy." A "T" limitation might be "We're overworked; we need another person or two." An "S" limitation might be "Our budget won't be finalized until after the due date on the project."

After all have finished their PTS notes (that is, to continue the medical analogy, the "diagnosis" part of the game), all notes should be posted on a wall (whiteboard) or in the center of the table. They can be mixed up, in no particular order. Now all team members get up and view the assembled limitations. The final objective is to dialogue about how to overcome the identified limitations, that is, to write the "prescription" to deal with the therapy.

In order to do this, the next strategy of the game is for each team member to choose 3 PTS notes from the wall or table that are not his or her own, and caucus with the person who wrote them in dialogue about how to overcome those specific limitations. This process

Notes

will obviously take two iterations, since each person needs to choose and to be chosen. Let there be an element of choice to this, even if it takes more time. Reflecting on someone else's thoughts about limitations is time well spent.

Discussion Questions

Facilitate a general discussion after the dialogues. Ask what we can do to address these limitations. Are there any that can be combined? Which would you say are the most severe limitations? Which have the greatest effect on our short-range goals? Our long-range goals?

Physically re-post the self-stick notes in related groups and talk about the relationships. Use this game to begin a creative thinking process for dealing with obstacles and limitations.

Remember in dialogue to work through obstacles by listening actively and responding as a collaborator. Refer to games 46, 47, and 48 for more information on dialogue.

Materials

Stacks of 3×3-inch self-stick note pads.

Approximate Time Required

45–60 minutes.

73
Job Modeling

Objective

To revisit the structure of one's job, using the people-data-things model of job analysis.

Procedure

At a team meeting early in the life of a team (within the first 3 to 6 months), ask team members to take a few minutes to reflect upon what they actually do as team members. Using the Department of Labor "people-data-things" job analysis model, ask each team member to list the things he or she actually does in each category.

This generally can be done on one piece of paper, in this manner: Fold the paper in thirds vertically, making three columns. Open the paper, flatten the folds, and write a heading for each column, that is, a People column, a Data column, and a Things column. Ask team members to reflect upon what they actually do (not what their job description says) on the job and post those elements of the job in the appropriate columns.

After they see the contrasting lengths of the three columns, ask them to give a rough percentage estimate of their actual jobs. What percentage of the job is people tasks? What percentage of the job is data tasks? What percentage of the job is things tasks? Remember, they should add up to 100 percent.

Discussion Questions

Most folks try to do the things that are written in their job descriptions, or that were printed in the want ad that advertised their job. That's often as far as anyone goes in "modeling" the job. This exercise helps folks think about their actual jobs, and create models of them that can be useful for determining learning requirements for the immediate and long-range future.

Simply ask team members to recreate their jobs on paper according to the

Notes

people-data-things model. If they are having trouble getting started, suggest that they think about a team goal, a personal challenge, a specific product and their role in its creation, a particular requirement of membership on this team, what they've gotten rewarded for in the past, or the low-level skills and the high-level skills they are expected to use.

With today's focus on performance and the reorganization of work into teams, often the bewildered employee doesn't seem to know what his or her job really is. This reflective and analytical job modeling technique can be helpful, especially after a few months of working as a team.

Materials

Pencils and paper.

Approximate Time Required

30–45 minutes.

74
Disturbing the Peace

Objective

To practice "pattern-breaking thinking,"
that is, instead of keeping the peace, team
members will disturb the peace.

Procedure

This is an exercise in thinking in a different way. It takes only a few minutes, but can have a dramatic effect of jolting one's present train of thought into new directions. This is the kind of thinking required for service and product innovation. Pattern-breaking thinking is a skill that can be learned and must be practiced. This is an exercise in practice.

Take a few minutes at any time during a team meeting or training session to focus the team's attention on concepts that can be refocused simply by changing the form of the words in them, or by expressing them with related words that mean the opposite of the original intent of the concept. Disturbing the peace is an example; it is what is truly desired in an innovative work environment, although keeping the peace is what employees often think they should be doing. Intellectual disturbance, not stasis, is what generally leads to innovation—a breaking from the traditionalist pattern of thinking.

Simply call out or write on a whiteboard a dichotomy like "keeping the peace"/"disturbing the peace." Cross out the word "keeping" and replace it with the word "disturbing." Think of one or two more and start the team thinking about their additions to your short list.

Discussion Questions

Keep the exercise going long enough for at least half of the team to contribute. Suggest that pattern-breaking thinking is useful, desirable, and the gate to creativity and innovation. Here are some other examples:

Notes

- the pursuit of happiness ... the happiness of pursuit

- seeing the unseen

- comfort the afflicted ... afflict the comfortable

- hope is not that things will turn out well, but that they will make sense no matter how they turn out (Sherwin B. Nuland, MD, *How We Die,* 1994 National Book Award Winner. NY: Vintage, 1994).

Thanks to the Rev. Shawnthea Monroe of the Trinitarian Congregational Church, Concord, MA for the inspiration for this exercise. She is good at pattern-breaking thinking ... and at afflicting the comfortable.

Materials

Whiteboard and markers.

Approximate Time Required

5–10 minutes.

75

City on a Hill

Objective

To demonstrate two different approaches to the same "futuring" task, one using forward-looking images and the other using backward-looking images.

Procedure

Divide the team into two subteams for the purpose of writing a mock campaign speech, in which the speaker is seeking election as a leader of the team. Model it on a speech-writing process and a speech much as a presidential candidate might deliver during a campaign. Assign one subteam to a forward-looking approach and the other subteam to a backward-looking approach. Ask each subteam to choose a recorder who will take notes. Focus on getting the speech outlined in its entirety, with key campaign phrases specified. However, the speech does not have to be written in final form. This is an exercise in contrasting ways of expressing the same idea, not in speech writing. After the writing, share each perspective with the entire team. Suggest ways in which the team could adapt each approach; discuss pros and cons of each approach as a means of imagining the future.

Discussion Questions

Team members might be helped by remembering the presidential race between Bill Clinton and Bob Dole during 1996. Both candidates wanted to convey to voters a hope for a better future—the same sort of goal that many companies have when they organize themselves into teams. Bob Dole, the older and more experienced public servant, chose to focus on the image of his home in "Kansas back then" and of other past successes of his leadership; Bill Clinton chose to create the image of a "bridge to the twenty-first century," and to spell out simply what every 12-year-old, every 8-year-old, and every family would be able to do after crossing that bridge. They were two very different ways of

Notes

creating images of the future and of their leadership approaches. Each approach had appeal, but each was different from the other in the images it used and evoked. Talk about this campaign, so that team members can see the differences in image-making and the use of words to create those images.

Ask subteam members to create images to support each subteam's perspective as they campaign for leadership.

Make this as long an exercise as you have time for; extend it by having actual copies of a Dole and a Clinton campaign speech for each subteam member. Give all persons a copy of each speech, so that they can see what each was and was not, and can see differences. Make the speech writing itself into more of a finished product instead of just an outline with key words. Extend the exercise into one of delivering the speech. Debrief the entire process if you have plenty of time.

Materials

Knowledge of two different campaign speeches, or copies of speeches such as those by Bob Dole and Bill Clinton in the 1996 presidential election campaign.

Approximate Time Required

30–60 minutes.

76
"I Have a Dream"

Objective

To illustrate the power of a theme or a vision rather than a plan.

Procedure

Get a copy of a famous speech, for example, Dr. Martin Luther King's "I Have a Dream" speech at the Lincoln Memorial in Washington, DC on August 28, 1963. Find it in your local library or by contacting the Martin Luther King, Jr. Center for Nonviolent Social Change in Atlanta, GA. Make copies for all team members and analyze it as if you were in a high school English class. Use highlighter pens and make notes in the margin as you go through it. Illustrate the "creativity" principle that overarching themes or visions can move action forward at least as much as strategic plans.

Discussion Questions

Ask team members to read through the speech and search for the themes or the vision statements. Ask them to analyze the speech to find the loaded words that evoke deep understanding. Some of these are:

> "rise from the dark and desolate valley of segregation …"

> "drinking not from the cup of bitterness and hatred…."

> "You have been veterans of creative suffering …"

> "one day every valley shall be exalted … and all flesh shall see it together"

King has been called perhaps the greatest man of the twentieth century, not so much for his intellectual brilliance as for his ability to articulate a vision that earned him the trust of both whites, who saw him as operating in good faith and blacks, who saw him as not selling out black interests. He reinvigorated oratory as a means of mobilizing forces,

Notes

and his speeches are worth studying to see just how his verbal images, metaphors, and connections with the spiritual underpinnings of society were combined in very effective messages and motivations.

King, of course, was connected through his family of preachers to the National Baptist Convention, and therefore to a large core of like-minded people. He could have chosen strategic planning as a precursor to change. Instead, he chose oratory that skillfully tapped into the deep understandings of both black and white Christians. Approach this exercise as you would a literature analysis assignment. Good oratory uses creative design and delivery conventions. Often oratory works when planning fails, because it taps into a deeper well of understanding and evokes a more creative and often more powerful response.

> The story goes that Jack Welch, CEO of General Electric, threw out his strategic planning organization and created visions instead. Welch is well-known for his monthly "pit" meetings, at which he stood in the pit of a lecture-hall amphitheater at a corporate training center and gave "sermons" about his empowerment vision known as "Work Out." Like King, Welch discovered the power of charged and connected words that reached resoundingly and deeply into the hearers' visions of themselves. (See *The Witch Doctors* by John Micklethwait and Adrian Wooldridge, NY: Times Books/Random House, 1996, pp. 150ff.)

Materials

A copy of the "I Have a Dream" speech by Dr. Martin Luther King, Jr., August 28, 1963, Washington, DC.

Approximate Time Required

20–40 minutes.

77
Think-*ing*

Objective

To jolt team members into a more active way of thinking.

Procedure

This is a task for the team leader or trainer. During a team meeting or training session, interrupt team members in discussion and change their use of nouns into "… ing" verbs. For example, whenever anyone says "management," you say "manag *ing*." People engaged in change often rail at some objectified "thing," making it a target for blame, as in "Management around here stinks."

If such words are turned into active words, the meaning changes and becomes a living process, something to be played with, manipulated, engaged in, or made better. Play this little word game for half an hour or so, until you make the point that the simple trick of thinking in terms of "… ing" words can lead to process improvement much more quickly because "… ing" thinking already puts one in an action frame of mind.

Discussion Questions

Here are some other typical targets you'll find in standard business talk. Listen for these and others like them; ask team members to reorient their thinking from noun to verb, object to process.

> service (serving)
>
> communication (communicating)
>
> leadership (leading)
>
> commitment (committing)
>
> design (designing)
>
> investment (investing)
>
> work (working)
>
> development (developing)
>
> reflection (reflecting)
>
> improvement (improving)

Notes

There are, of course, many variations of this game that are possible: It can be done as a pencil and paper exercise, team members can work in pairs to catch each other, it can be turned into a flip chart exercise in which the leader writes down every "noun" that can be turned into a "verb," etc.

Materials

None.

Approximate Time Required

15–20 minutes.

78

Crystal Ball

Objective

To engage in envisioning the future through imagining various future scenarios; to tease out of current trends and circumstances the potential needs for new technologies and business policies.

Procedure

Go to a kids' toy store and buy a clear vinyl pool or beach ball, one about 10 inches in diameter—one with sparkles on it would be just fine. This will be your team's crystal ball.

At a team meeting or training session, introduce the subject of creating future scenarios. Tell the team that you're going to play a "What if...?" game for the next few minutes. Ask them to imagine what some future(s) might be like for this company 10 years, 20 years, and 50 years from now (or any one of these, for a shorter game). Ask them to think specifically about two kinds of things: (1) policies or mission statements, and (2) technologies. You might want to give the team members a choice of working on either (1) or (2), since some people are more naturally drawn to either but not both. Giving participants a choice also shortens the game.

Write on a flip chart or whiteboard these four categories:

Work Processes

Output: Services

Output: Products

Company Name

These are the areas for consideration in creating future scenarios; each team member will think about the stated future time (e.g., 20 years from now) in terms of all four of these. Pose the questions, "What will work processes look like at this company in 20 years?" "What will services look like in 20 years?" "What will products look like in 20 years?" and "What will the company name be in 20 years?"

To start the game, pick up the crystal ball and toss it to the first person, who

221

Notes

will handle it for a few seconds and reply to the four questions. Then that person will toss it to anyone else in the room for the second person to likewise answer the four questions. The process of toss and answer continues until all team members have had a turn at "crystal ball" reading.

Discussion Questions

Remind the team to "parallel process" as they are creating their scenarios in each of the four categories; that is, they should be thinking about policies and missions as well as technologies as they think about each of the four categories.

> This is a complex game in that it contains a challenge to each person's processing power, both right-brain and left-brain challenges; a strong and tangible metaphor; and the element of surprise. It can take only a few minutes, but it can truly exercise one's creative skills.

Materials

Whiteboard or flip chart and marker.

Approximate Time Required

10–45 minutes.

79

Fashion Show

Objective

To enable team members to vent frustration at "management fads" of the past; to surface the old models in order to suggest the new ones.

Procedure

This is a game to be played at a multi-team social event or companywide conference of teams. It is meant to be a spoof on the company's favorite ideas—some of which worked and some of which didn't work. This will be a good energizer, so it could be done at a normally "down" time like right before or after mid-afternoon break. It also makes a fun sideshow during lunch.

Each team selects a management fad as the one it will represent in a fashion show. Much as a team might build a float to enter into a parade, this team will dress up one of its members as a management fad and "parade down the runway," fashion show style, with the other team entries. Crazy hats, wild T-shirts, signs, papier mâché creations, all would be appropriate. Announce the start of the Fashion Show with music and/or the overhead on page 225. Make a big deal of it if your room has a stage and spotlights, or if you can create a runway through the middle of the luncheon tables. Make it look like a fashion show. Have an announcer at a microphone who can introduce each team and who can lead the applause after each entry.

Discussion Questions

None.

Notes

> Management theory is full of fads, some of which work and some of which don't work. People who work in teams often get subjected to an unusually large number of "try-this-and-see-if-it-works" ideas. Team members need opportunities to let off steam, perhaps more than other employees do. This game is one way to do this.

Materials

Music, microphone, overhead (see page 225).

Approximate Time Required

Several hours preparation time; 20 minutes show time.

Fashion Show

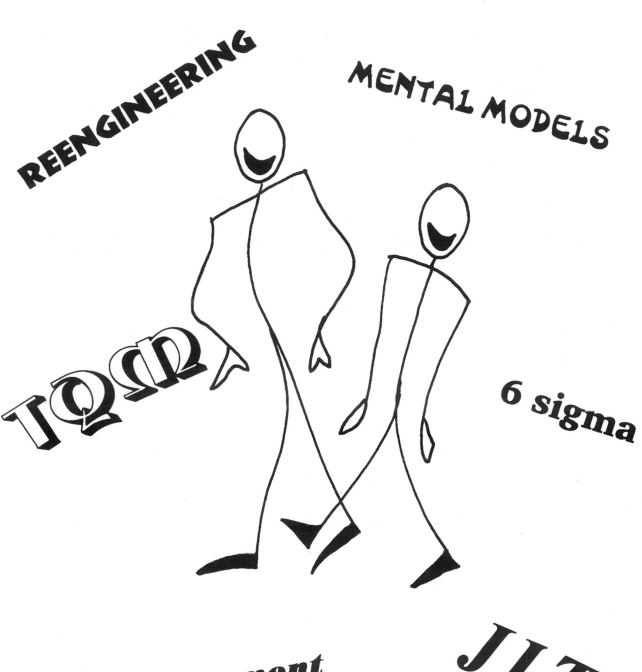

REENGINEERING

MENTAL MODELS

TQM

6 sigma

Empowerment

JIT

80
Expert System

Objective

To engage team members in thinking about what experts do and how they do it.

Procedure

Make a copy of the handout on page 229 for each team member. Hand it out at the start of this exercise. Tell the team that this paper, that is, these two lists, represents an "expert system"— one list contains creative behaviors; the other list contains areas of work requiring expert behavior. Tell the team that the experts under consideration already have the technical skills to do the job, but they sometimes lack initiative in the creative behaviors that would truly make their work an expert system. Suggest that the team combine terms from each list to lead the way toward that expert system. Do this as a brainstorming kind of exercise, allowing anyone who has an idea to simply call it out.

Discussion Questions

Before you begin, you might want to familiarize the team with the "Areas of Work" list by having them suggest which five terms are the ones most relevant to the work of the team. This will get them to scan the entire list and begin to prioritize the items in the list. Alphabetizing the list is a technique for mixing up the content, forcing people to think harder about the concepts they're dealing with.

Notes

Add any terms to either list that better reflect your own team.

Materials

Copies of handout for each team member (see page 229).

Approximate Time Required

30 minutes.

Expert System

CREATIVE BEHAVIORS

alter	recombine	simplify
arrange	reconstruct	simulate
change	regroup	synthesize
combine	rename	value
design	reorganize	vary
generalize	reorder	
modify	restate	
paraphrase	restructure	
question	revise	
rearrange	rewrite	

AREAS OF WORK REQUIRING EXPERT BEHAVIOR

demonstration	management	reasoning
elaboration	memory and recall	self-esteem
estimation	muscle coordination	speed
evaluation	organization	translation
independent thinking	oral/verbal expression	visualizing
inference	prioritizing	writing

81
Clouds

Objective

To watch clouds forming and moving, as a metaphor for understanding the definition of a "self-organizing system."

Procedure

Do this brief focusing exercise at an off-premises workshop or while walking outdoors for a lunch break. Simply pick a day when the sky is full of moving and changing clouds and lead the team in watching them move and change for a few minutes. Suggest to the team that clouds seem to be a nearly perfect self-organizing system, clouds being independent and interdependent at once—dynamic, creative, and free to adapt to their environment.

Discussion Questions

Help team members see that teams can be like clouds, but only if they adopt a cloud-like approach, that is, an approach to their environment that recognizes that stasis and equilibrium are the temporary states. The more likely—and more creative—approach to one's environment is to value the dynamic and adaptive behaviors that drive change.

Lead a discussion of various work environments (e.g., the technological environment, the human resources environment, the financial environment, the public relations environment, etc.) and what "clouds" might have to say in each example.

Notes

Two books on the subject are: Gareth Morgan's *Images of Organization,* Newbury Park, CA: Sage Publications, 1986, viz. chapter 3; and Margaret Wheatley's *Leadership and the New Science,* San Francisco: Berrett-Koehler, 1992/94, viz. chapter 5.

Materials

None, except a sky full of clouds.

Approximate Time Required

10–15 minutes.

82
Play Ball!

Objective

To determine the various roles for team players in several kinds of sports teams; to draw analogies to work teams.

Procedure

Do this exercise at a wall that has at least two standard whiteboards mounted on it, so that at least four team members can work at the board side by side.

Before the team assembles, prepare the whiteboard with four columns, each headed by the title of a sport that uses a ball, for example: column 1, football; column 2, basketball; column 3, tennis doubles; column 4, baseball.

Then ask for four volunteers to come to the board and each stand in front of one of the ball games. Their task is to think about how each of these games is played, and specifically about how the one game which they are standing in front of is played. Ask them to concentrate on the roles of the players (pitcher, catcher, shortstop, guard, forward, quarterback, fullback, net player, back player, etc.) Ask them to write down the roles of the various players on their ball team. Then ask the four volunteers to sit down.

Discussion Questions

Now direct the attention of the entire team to the information on the whiteboard. Ask the group if they can see the differences between the types of teams. Ask them if they can describe how interactions among team members occur. Ask them if their own team is more like one team or another, or if it is really like a combination of "ways to play ball"—or if it is analogous to some other kind of sport team entirely (e.g., swim team or track team).

Notes

Too often executives or managers who are pushing for teams don't have a clue about what kind of teams they want in their workplaces. Teams often form without much guidance or understanding of roles and organizational models. This exercise can help in defining the team, especially the roles each player is expected to play.

Materials

Whiteboards and markers.

Approximate Time Required

20–30 minutes.

83

A Better Game

Objective

To introduce the elements of game theory as a variant of or foil for strategic planning.

Procedure

This exercise introduces the team to the elements of game theory and the concept of "co-opetition" (Brandenburger and Nalebuff, 1996), a combination of cooperation and competition in order to make the game more fun.

Team members will be familiar with the mental model of competition in game playing, the winning and losing mentality of most sports' teams. Most team members, however, will not be familiar or comfortable with the idea of cooperation in order for the *playing* to be more interesting. It's that idea this exercise addresses. In addition, the nature of game playing is often the cognitive organizer or trigger that is necessary to help folks restructure what they've just learned in order to integrate it into their experiences more completely and more easily. The point is to define a bigger pie, a greater game, so that everyone's play is much more interesting and everyone's piece is potentially larger.

Discussion Questions

In this exercise, ask team members to focus on a key product or service that has made the company famous or wealthy. Ask them then to consider how a competitor's similar product could be adapted for some business use within your company. For example, could it be used in an advertisement together with your own product? Could it be purchased and sold at a discount together with your product as a "duo of excellence"? Could its features be used to highlight not only its own but also your product's features?

Notes

Current voices are being heard that advocate seemingly radical new ways of thinking. One such voice is the voice of many who say that "strategic planning" has become a relatively useless business function and that visioning seems to produce better results; another voice says, "throw out the hierarchies and levels." Finally, there is the author's voice, saying that win–win is much more fun than win–lose.

Materials

None.

Approximate Time Required

30 minutes.

84
Mindmapping

Objective

To create a mindmap.

Procedure

A mindmap is an associative representation using words and graphic elements in such a way as to facilitate memory. Mindmapping has been used also to identify and describe a network of interconnected elements. Mindmapping has been a useful tool both at work and in personal life.

A mindmap starts with a nucleus, a center, often graphic in nature (e.g., a star, a heart, a dollar sign, an arrow, a smiley face, a key). Underlined printed words generally accompany connecting links. A finished mindmap resembles a spider web, a tree, a map, or a brain cell.

Begin the exercise by asking team members to create a mindmap entitled "Retirement." Any concept of retirement is acceptable—planning for retirement, avoiding retirement, enjoying retirement, and any other variations are just fine. Ask each team member to draw his or her own personal "Retirement" mindmap (see sample on page 239).

Ground rules are simple:

- Start with a center word or symbol.
- Connect all strands together.
- Use graphic elements such as size of letters, shading and outlining, upper and lower case, spacing and crowding, lines and shapes, different colors, etc.
- Use keywords.
- Print all words.
- Underline each word.
- Use symbols liberally.

Share finished Retirement Mindmaps with the group.

Discussion Questions

Suggest to team members that mindmapping mirrors the natural process of connection and communication in our brains, and that this is an exercise in "bringing the global into the local." Ask team members to tell you about their mindmaps, particularly focusing on their thought processes during the development of connections. Ask for their feedback on the process of mindmapping; ask for a comparison of this process to a standard planning process with milestones, timelines, etc. Ask if the mindmapping process is adaptable to any team project.

> This approach to mindmapping follows the ideas of Tony Buzan at the College of Advanced Reading in England. His approach to the psychology of memory was sparked by observations of students taking notes and dialogues with them about how they used their notes. He found that greater and more associative elements created a greater ability to re-member. Symbols and pictures must be used in order to spark your imagination and enhance memory. Buzan believes that thinking processes can be improved by modeling the neurological, natural processes of the brain. Mindmapping is brain-friendly.

Materials

Unlined paper and plenty of colored markers of various point sizes for each team member.

Approximate Time Required

30–45 minutes.

Mindmapping

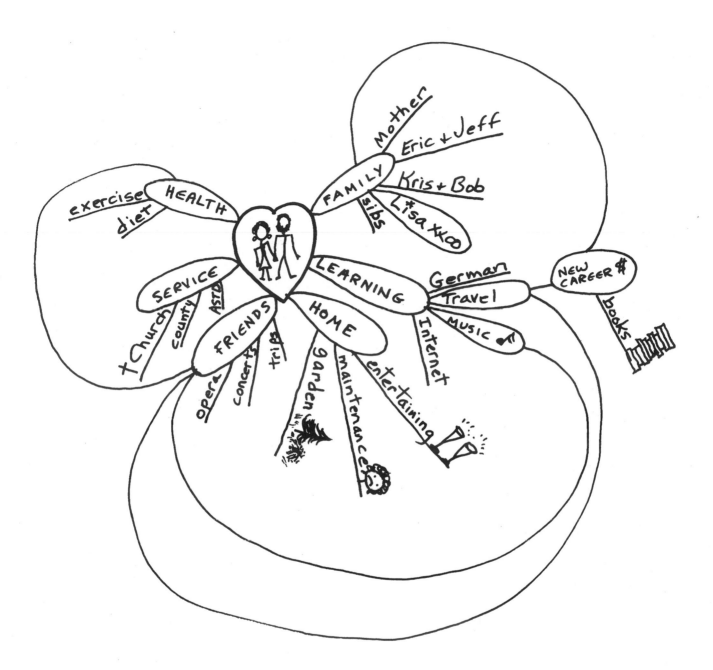

85

Friendly Robots

Objective

To learn the basic guidelines for creating online teaching games.

Procedure

This is not a game: It is a lesson in creating particular kinds of games. These are parts of the instructional games played online or through CBT software packages. Sometimes they are known as "intelligent tutors"; here we'll call them "Friendly Robots." They are features of a larger instructional program that typically includes problems to solve, branching to related information sources, and online "lectures," often through a video clip. The gaming feature of instructional technology is sometimes overlooked in the seriousness of applying a standard instructional design methodology.

Friendly Robots should be envisioned as having smiley faces, swift and gentle giants poised to do the cognitive bidding of the master at the keypad and of the learning system behind the keypad. Students consistently tell designers that intelligent tutors should not only be right, they should also be fun.

These are some of the basic guidelines for Friendly Robots. Make a copy for each team member to use in discussion (copy page 243 as a handout).

1. Let robots do the grunt work, for example, the square roots, adding up long columns of figures, labeling, spell checking, and other low-level tasks not part of the specific objectives of the lesson.

2. Robots should appear every now and then and show their happy faces; CBT should not be dull and full of words.

3. Robots should help to create the right game for the right environment; for example, a game with problem-solving objectives must feature robots who engage the learner in problem-solving behavior.

Notes

4. Robots should monitor the play, assessing and measuring the learner's responses, motivating the learner in the process of learning with surface interventions as needed based on the monitoring.

5. Robots should deliver the feedback and deliver it often—winning, losing, truth, fiction, good choices and bad choices, errors and scores.

6. Robots should always help to carry the instruction through the playing of the game.

Discussion Questions

Refer to the handout (page 243), item by item. Ask team members to interject their own "mini case studies" about their experiences of learning online. Start with the simple "help" commands or "spell checker" found on most PCs. Relate the team members' experiences directly to each of the six items to help them understand what these guidelines are saying. See if team members have specific ideas for making their own learning online more effective.

Work of the Learning Technology Institute, Warrenton, VA has been on the leading edge of design of instruction delivery systems and interactive instruction development. The Institute's publications typically contain articles on current issues in the field. Research relevant to "Robot Assistants" was reported by John Leddo in LTI's Fall 1996 *Journal of Instruction Delivery Systems*, pp. 22–25.

Materials

Handouts for each team member (see page 243).

Approximate Time Required

20 minutes.

Friendly Robots

☐ **1.** Let robots do the grunt work, for example, the square roots, adding up long columns of figures, labeling, spell checking, and other low-level tasks not part of the specific objectives of the lesson.

☐ **2.** Robots should appear every now and then and show their happy faces; CBT should not be dull and full of words.

☐ **3.** Robots should help to create the right game for the right environment; for example, a game with problem-solving objectives must feature robots who engage the learner in problem-solving behavior.

☐ **4.** Robots should monitor the play, assessing and measuring the learner's responses, motivating the learner in the process of learning with surface interventions as needed based on the monitoring.

☐ **5.** Robots should deliver the feedback and deliver it often—winning, losing, truth, fiction, good choices and bad choices, errors and scores.

☐ **6.** Robots should always help to carry the instruction through the playing of the game.

86
Open Up

Objective

To practice and critique the rules of brainstorming.

Procedure

Brainstorming is a more familiar name for divergent thinking, the kind of "left-field" thinking that is often practiced in training sessions—and left there. It is not the kind of thinking that people at work are accustomed to practicing because it has often been viewed as off the mark, inefficient, a diversion from the real work, or just plain silly.

One of the critical elements of divergent thinking is that it is generally described from the initiator's point of view, that is, what a person must do to be a divergent thinker. Another point of view is that of the receiver or observer—sometimes the harshest critic. This exercise is not so much about the divergent thinker as it is about the receiver of the efforts of divergent thinking; not about the primary actor but rather about the secondary actor in a brainstorming situation.

Choose a typical work problem that needs to be solved. Here are some possibilities: overuse of the copy machine, an annoying abundance of signoffs, too much playing with computers, too little space in the employee parking lot, too little choice at lunch. Apply the simple rules of brainstorming to the problem and ask the team to try to solve it following the rules of brainstorming. These are the rules:

1. **(Quantity)** Quantity of ideas is what counts; the more the better.

2. **(Connect)** Connect all ideas so that no one owns a particular idea; all participants own the composite.

3. **(Crazy)** Unconventional ideas and words are desirable; the sillier and crazier the better.

Notes

4. **(Suspend)** Suspend judgment; don't criticize any ideas, including your own.

5. **(Fuel)** Keep adding fuel; continue the process so that everyone participates.

These can be abbreviated and the keywords placed on a flip chart or whiteboard as a guide to the exercise and discussion afterward.

Discussion Questions

Now debrief the process of problem solving through divergent thinking which the team has just demonstrated to themselves. Focus on the momentary nonparticipant, the person who listened, who tried to become inspired to contribute, who was shy, or who simply hates to be pressured into doing anything, especially into thinking in a certain way. Ask the team what they needed in order to Open Up to engaging in divergent thinking. It's really the secondary persons in the brainstorming process who need the help. Use this exercise as an opportunity to set some ground rules for that part of brainstorming.

> Brainstorming has been around for a long time, but few people have focused on the secondary participant. If teams are to truly work together, concepts such as focus on "the other" must be a regular part of team skill-building. This is one such skill-building lesson.

Materials

Whiteboard or flip chart and markers.

Approximate Time Required

30 minutes.

87
Castle

Objective

To distinguish between features and benefits.

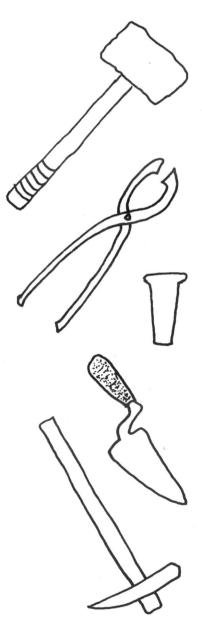

Procedure

Find a children's fable or classic story in which a variety of people are working together to build something or to cause something to happen. Another source would be the David Macaulay children's books on building pyramids, skyscrapers, cathedrals, mills, cities, etc. (Boston: Houghton Mifflin). Macaulay's *Castle* (1977) was the inspiration for this game. Make up your own story based on these sources.

This game makes the same point about perspective as the well-known fable of the blind men and the elephant, in which each blind man, not knowing the scope of the whole of the animal, touches a part of it and declares the "object" a tree (leg), a snake (trunk), a wall (its side). In this game, however, the player is required to see from two perspectives, that of "features" and that of "benefits."

Jobs, tasks, systems, procedures, and projects all have both features and benefits. Most of us find it easier to "see" the more tangible "features" and focus on enhancing those features; it is harder to see the more intangible "benefits." However, it's generally the benefits that translate to success, profit, and value.

The game starts with a story. At key points, stop the story and ask team members, "Why is he or she doing that?" or, "What is that for?" Record answers on a whiteboard or flip chart in either a Features column or a Benefits column. Continue the story and the two questions until most of the responses fall into the Benefits column.

A story might go something like this: An assortment of laborers, some three thousand strong, was required to build the castle on Limestone Point. Eric, a quarryman, when asked why he was dig-

Notes

ging, said, "To get fine round stones" (Features column). Kris, another quarryman, when asked the same question, said, "To make a roadway" (Benefits column).

Continue on, elaborating on the workers (blacksmith, mortar maker, master mason, carpenter, digger, etc), their work, and their responses to the questions.

Discussion Questions

During discussion, be sure that team members see the difference between responses listed in the Features column and those in the Benefits column. Continue the discussion by "framing" a team project in the same storyline as the game story, including the work of various team members, identifying their work and them by name. Ask each team member the two key questions, "Why are you doing that?" and "What is that for?" Identify responses as either Features or Benefits, steering the responses toward the Benefits designation.

Help team members in their thinking about benefits by suggesting that benefits, that is, value-added products and services, are why your company is in business. Most employees are so narrowly concerned with their own jobs that they only see the parameters of their own personal work. They need practice in thinking beyond the descriptions of their results to the larger business needs of the company.

Materials

A good story; whiteboard or flip chart and marker.

Approximate Time Required

30–60 minutes.

88
Oracle

Objective

To experience the results of chance, through the game of runes.

Procedure

Runes are a set of 21 small stones each marked with a glyph or letter-type symbol representing life characteristics, for example, strength, constraint, defense, opening, growth, standstill, breakthrough, wholeness, joy, and others. They are part of Viking history and folklore; they are akin to an oracle which one consults in times of stress or searching. Like all oracles, runes can be a mirror of one's inner self. A sample of rune symbols appears on page 251.

Oracles have been a part of Western thinking for centuries; the most famous oracle was the Oracle at Delphi, Greece, whose admonition was to "Know thyself." Oracles can teach us through reaching into the inward self at moments of readiness, beyond or beneath "designed" or "structured" learning. Adding the dimension of a game, as in Reading Runes or Casting Runes, can free the player from the disciplines and strictures of reasoned thought. Runes, like horoscopes or fortune cookies, can break through to one's most receptive self.

Runes are available in game stores and catalogs. To play, you'll need to purchase a set of runes and a guidebook to their use. The simplest game of runes is the Draw One Rune overview game, in which a person picks one rune out of a bag. Another is Casting Runes, in which all 21 runes are cast out upon a rune field (napkin or small rug or packed down area of earth), and the runes with the glyph side up are read. Runes are read according to a key that matches the glyph to a traditional meaning for that symbol.

Notes

Discussion Questions

When runes are to be read, the question to ask is, "What can my intuitive self say about the message of this rune in relationship to my present situation?"

Conditioning, habit, and rules of logical thought often keep folks "in the box." "Out-of-the-box thinking" has been a rallying cry during this present age of empowered employees. Games of runes and other oracle consultations can reach into a more malleable and open part of one's thinking, leading to out-of-the-box learning and creativity.

Materials

A bag of runes and a guidebook to their use.

Approximate Time Required

1–2 minutes per person for Draw One Rune; 5 minutes per person for Casting Runes.

Examples of Runes

From Ralph Blum, *The Book of Runes,* London: Headline Book Publishing, 1993.

STRENGTH

CONSTRAINT

BREAKTHROUGH

MOVEMENT

WHOLENESS

STANDSTILL

FLOW

89

Vices of the Virtual

Objective

To differentiate information presented in books versus information presented through hypertext online.

Procedure

This is a simple listing exercise, complex because of the newness of the concept of "virtual" context. People often don't stop to reflect upon just exactly what information consumerism is all about these days. This exercise forces that reflection. Too often, in the rush to learn how to access information online, we forget to stop and think about what it is we are accessing. In the rush to "how" we neglect the all-important, fundamental "what."

Do this as a flip chart or whiteboard exercise, in which team members simply call out descriptors that fall in either column, "Physical Book" or "Virtual Book." Try to get them to think of opposites; that is, when they come up with a term for one column, try to get them at the same time to state its counterpart, opposite, or related term for the other column. "Physical book" refers to the kind of book we're all used to holding in our hands, leafing through the physical pages of, and keeping on our desks or bookshelves. "Virtual book" refers to a body of information created through hypertext technology. Remind team members that *http* stands for hypertext transfer protocol.

Here are some examples, for starters:

Virtual: scrolled, inductive, mutable, repackaged, slippery

Physical: leafed, deductive, static, finite, firm

Discussion Questions

Focus on the nature of information from each source; tell team members to think of themselves as "information consumers." Any descriptors they think of are acceptable; it's fine to start with

Notes

features of either. If they get stuck in system or book descriptors only, lead them into a more precise focus on the nature of the information produced by either type of "book." Ask them how that feature affects the information resulting from it. Keep the comparing and contrasting going as long as anyone has any more ideas. This is a stretch exercise.

Online learning and online communication are becoming more and more a reality for many teams who are separated from each other either across buildings, states, or continents. Since information is the common denominator for networked teams, team members need to pause occasionally and define just what is the nature of that information, if they like it that way, and what actions might be needed to modify or enhance its quality.

Just as discerning consumers of print-on-paper information need to sort out the effects of edited news, personal opinion, propaganda, advertisement, and filtered stories, consumers of online information must likewise become discerning consumers of their kind of information.

It has been said that in using the Net, you find only what you're looking for. That certainly puts a great deal of emphasis and responsibility on the searcher to be mentally fit, motivated in the right directions, and creative. Authors writing for Net consumers worry about preserving the integrity of their ideas and their writing; they worry about the capacity of the tool of hypertext linkages to change the original work through creation of many contexts in which to see the original work, which then becomes "original plus."

Advocates of the "virtual book" say that assembling knowledge and turning it into learning is enhanced by the unexpected insight that comes from the process of accessing information online. This exercise can help your team to stretch their mental muscles in discernment.

Materials

Whiteboard or flip chart and marker.

Approximate Time Required

30–45 minutes.

90

Hypertext Hurdles

Objective

To play a devil's advocate game of creating "What if...?" scenarios with hypertext information in the area of team evaluation.

Procedure

This is a mind game, playing "What if...?" with team evaluation standards. The setting is online information. That is, all information that is usable in the various scenarios of the game must come from online sources. Play begins as team members one by one think of an online scenario in which the focused nature of hypertext searching omitted something critical or compromised a source somehow. In other words, this is a game purposely imagining particular potential problems in meeting evaluation standards because of online searching. Often, imagining what problems could occur helps to prevent them. Often, too, defining what "bad things" might be makes the "good things" all the more obvious.

Start by making a copy of the Team Evaluation Standards, page 257, for each team member. Give them a few minutes to read through them, or read them aloud together for added emphasis. (This game can be played using any kinds of standards, for example, course development standards, product development or quality standards, standards for writing newspaper or journal articles, etc.)

Play should progress in order, one by one, around the room. The first team member addresses standard #1, the second team member addresses standard #2, and so on. It could go something like this:

☐ 2. **Clarity of results.** *What if* the keyboarder made a mistake in identifying the x and y axes and the graph was actually backwards? It looked great, but made no sense.

Notes

☐ **3. Communication.** *What if* I chose e-mail as a communication delivery system and half of my list of names get so much e-mail that they've turned off to it and read only short messages from friends?

Go around the room, one by one, until all have taken a turn at creating a "What if...?" scenario, going from standard to standard in order. If the creative juices are flowing, continue around the room again in the same manner, with a second round and a third round of scenarios for each standard.

Discussion Questions

Always challenge the responder to answer the "What if" question, drawing on his or her experience and on what is known or imagined about learning and communicating online. Encourage individualized responses, personalized by experience or beliefs about online learning or communication. Talk about the kinds of thinking skills required to effectively communicate and learn on the Net, as suggested by the responses to all of the "What if...?" questions during the game.

For some good reading on the subject of thinking and survival skills for Internet users, see Paul Gilster's book, *Digital Literacy,* New York: John Wiley, 1997.

Materials

Handouts for each team member (see page 257).

Approximate Time Required

20–30 minutes.

Hypertext Hurdles

TEAM EVALUATION STANDARDS

☐ 1. **Intent.** Have a plan of action for the use of results.

☐ 2. **Clarity of results.** Present results clearly, plausibly, avoiding jargon and acronyms. Check communication for user-friendliness.

☐ 3. **Communication.** Communicate widely to all stakeholders, that is, to all who will be affected by the results inside and outside of the team.

☐ 4. **Graphics.** Use simple graphic charts (bar, pie, timelines, etc.) to convey critical information; go easy on the statistical narrative text.

☐ 5. **First-person comments.** Use evaluator comments, verbatim. Quotes enliven otherwise "dead" presentation of data.

☐ 6. **Act, not react.** Recognize that all feedback is good, both positive and negative evaluations. Make failure your friend, learn from mistakes, and don't repeat them. Offensive, not defensive, is the word.

☐ 7. **Close the loop.** Use evaluation data as soon as possible, feeding it into a definition of new needs. Set new goals and timelines. Implement, monitor, and evaluate, again and again.

91
Tell Me a Different Story

Objective

To tell a favorite story in two different formats, one as if it were from a bound book, and the other as if it were constructed using hypertext online.

Procedure

This is a game mostly for the trainer or team leader. In it, you will tell a story in two different ways to your team, in order for them to see and hear the differences in "reading" requirements for each kind of storytelling.

Choose one of your favorite children's stories: Snow White, The Little Match Girl, Jack and the Beanstalk, The Little Engine That Could, The Velveteen Rabbit, The Three Little Pigs, Hans Brinker and the Silver Skates, or whatever. Tell the story much as you remember it from your childhood, as it appeared in your favorite book. Then tell the same story as if it were unfolding to you, the Internet reader, online, with all the wonders of hypertext linkages available to you.

Team members simply have to listen to the two versions of the story.

Discussion Questions

After the storytelling, ask the team to describe the kinds of reading skills required for each and how to acquire those skills; ask them what kinds of thinking skills are required for each kind of story.

Notes

> The advantages of hypertext have been well known for research and accessibility of a range of data. Net surfing, however, is not the same as reading a book. Lead your team through this game of storytelling into realizing the differences, and determining whether they have appropriate current skills for the type of "reading" or "learning" that they are required to do on the job.

Materials

None.

Approximate Time Required

1 hour preparation; 1 hour presentation.

92

Obstacle Course

Objective

To list obstacles to achieving process quality in the work of the team.

Procedure

This is a simple listing exercise, to be used at the beginning of a discussion or planning session on quality, that is, Total Quality Management (TQM) for teams.

Take a few minutes at the beginning of a discussion to call out several categories of "process quality" efforts. As you say each one, ask team members to suggest obstacles (organizational, managerial, educational, environmental, etc.) to carrying out that kind of effort. Record the responses on a flip chart or whiteboard.

Sometimes in a group setting, people are more open and likely to say things that might be misinterpreted as "whining" in a one-to-one interaction; the object here is for team members to *specify* what they see as getting in the way of progress. By making the exercise very specific and tied to different process quality goals, you increase the team's chances of carefully and correctly identifying obstacles that can be removed. Whining is generalized discontent; making it specific helps to remove the suspicion of whining and points you on your way to making improvements.

Discussion Questions

Ask the team to specify obstacles to achieving process quality, or as W. Edwards Deming said, "building quality in," in the following categories:

1. Constantly improving the system for production;

2. Constantly improving the system for service;

3. Conducting on-the-job training;

4. Driving out fear;

5. Eliminating hierarchical barriers;

6. Promoting career development and self-improvement.

Don't forget the quality movement as you develop teams. Deming's philosophy of building quality in, continuous improvement, and continuous learning are meant for teams. It's helpful to adopt the mind-set that mistakes and obstacles are learning opportunities and that all feedback is good.

Materials

Flip chart or whiteboard and marker.

Approximate Time Required

10–20 minutes.

93

Past Is Prologue

Objective

To value past achievements by team members while moving on with new work.

Procedure

At a team meeting, introduce new directions and new ideas about work processes by first doing this exercise which values your team members' past achievements. Go around the table, asking each team member in turn these questions:

1. What accomplishment(s) in your past working career do you value?

2. What was the original objective of that work?

3. What value did the company get from that work?

4. In what ways is that kind of objective still valid here?

Simply give each person a chance to talk about past successes before launching into a pep talk about changing everything. Write the four questions on a whiteboard or flip chart so all can be thinking about their responses before they speak.

Discussion Questions

Talk about the value and benefits of team members' past successes. It's too easy to drive change on the backs of perceived weaknesses; do your team a favor and acknowledge past accomplishments. Keep the discussion focused on value and benefits and don't get into a gripe session about what's wrong with the present.

Notes

> You never know when you'll need to form a link beyond the team in order to facilitate the team's work. This kind of exercise can help you learn where and how the past value was delivered. It's worth repeating several times per year.

Materials

Whiteboard or flip chart and marker.

Approximate Time Required

15 minutes.

94
If You Were CIO ...

Objective

To encourage team members to think more concretely about imagination.

Procedure

There's a new title cropping up in corporate America: Chief Imagination Officer (CIO). It goes along with another new breed of titles like Chief Knowledge Officer (CKO). In companies committed to working in teams, it would not be surprising to find both titles.

For this game, all of your team members will imagine that they are in line to become a CIO. You are interviewing each one to find out more about them. Go around the table, one by one, and ask just this one question:

> *"Where do you do your best imagining?"*

Discussion Questions

Team members should be asked to answer truthfully for themselves. The variety of responses will amaze you. Debrief the game by talking about groupings of responses (e.g., nature-related settings, sports or adventure settings, cozy home settings, music or art settings, Lone Ranger type settings, business-related settings, etc.). Help the team see that creativity has tangible triggers, and that there are many kinds of triggers.

Notes

> *Fast Company* magazine, April:May 1997, told of Gateway 2000 company's new CIO, a 34-year-old former Marketing Manager with a BS degree in Finance. When asked, he replied to the magazine's reporter that one of Gateway 2000's best imagination exercises was for a team leader to take off for a day with a group of employees and ask them what the "spotted cow box" means. His hope was that the spotted cow box would be able to communicate the same values to Gateway's customers around the globe. Imagining is a tool; teams need to figure out how to use it.

Materials

None.

Approximate Time Required

3–5 minutes.

95

Personal Trainer

Objective

To borrow the concepts of a personal trainer and apply them to team learning.

Procedure

As part of the follow-up to a major training session, workshop, or conference, institute the role of personal trainer for each team member. This can be done either through your company's training department or within the team itself. The example to set here is of personal trainers within the team.

When ideas are fresh and motivations tend to be strong toward the direction of change, it's a good time to add the element of support for the learning challenges ahead. Soon after the major training event, or as part of its final day, introduce the concept of each team member's having a personal trainer to help with implementation of new ideas, ways of working, or acquiring new skills. Like personal fitness trainers, personal trainers at work are trusted allies who know an individual's needs and can give honest feedback during practice. Personal trainers are part diagnostician and part coach.

Suggest that team members pair off and become each other's personal trainers for a defined period such as 3 months, after which time different pairings should occur for the next 3 months, and so forth. If you have an odd number, seek help from the training department to supply someone who is tuned in to the work of your team, or have the team leader drop out to even the pool.

Discussion Questions

Suggest that important help from a personal trainer can be given in these areas:

1. to listen and to observe,

2. to acclaim and value small accomplishments,

Notes

3. to give speedy and truthful feedback,

4. to mirror ideas, beliefs, approaches, and wishes, and to validate them with the "trainee,"

5. to encourage and support prudent risk taking,

6. to interpret the company from other perspectives for the "trainee,"

7. to suggest improvements and sources of learning, and

8. to be a confidante and continuous learning booster of the "trainee."

Much that we know about how adults learn has consistently indicated that adults like to get immediate feedback, like to learn from work at work, and like to express themselves and what they bring personally to the job through new challenges. A personal trainer can facilitate all of these things.

Materials

None.

Approximate Time Required

A few minutes of explanation; 3-month time periods for personal training.

96

Triple Self-Portrait

Objective

To draw a picture of yourself from three points of view, thereby encouraging a creative representation of personality characteristics.

Procedure

Get a copy of Norman Rockwell's *Triple Self-Portrait,* oil on canvas, *Saturday Evening Post,* February 13, 1960, cover, as an example of a Triple Self-Portrait. Inexpensive copies are available by phoning the Norman Rockwell Museum, Stockbridge, MA, (413) 298-4100, gift shop, or by making a copy from a *Post* cover in a public library archive. Show the picture to the team. Pass it around the room so that each team member can look at it closely.

In the classic and beloved Rockwell painting, the artist renders three versions of himself: a figure seated on a stool in front of an easel with his back to the viewer, a reflection of himself visible in a large mirror to the left of the painting, and a work-in-progress of his face on the easel. The face and shoulders of the artist in work clothes and spectacles are reflected in the large mirror, but the face painted on the canvas is more dapper, cleaned up, and sophisticated—the way the artist would like to be rendered. Thus, the "triple self-portrait." In true Norman Rockwell humor, the painter in the picture has not painted the image he saw in the mirror; and the artist, Norman Rockwell, has painted both reality and image in the same painting.

A "Triple Self-Portrait" game can serve to allow team members to let off steam, to spark their artistic creativity, and to generate some humor. Suggest that the three elements also be present in their Triple Self-Portraits. These, coded in the drawing on page 271, are:

- ☐ **1.** a back view of the artist,
- ☐ **2.** a mirror reflecting the front view of the artist, and
- ☐ **3.** a canvas on which the finished portrait is emerging.

Notes

Give each team member a piece of drawing paper, 11×14-inch or 16×20-inch. Have markers, crayons, and colored pencils and erasers available at a central location. Team members may use any medium for drawing: pencil, pen, markers, crayons, or colored pencils. Encourage any kind of figures—stick figures, cartoon-like figures, or figures drawn in three dimensions. The room in the picture may be obvious, and other props and decorations can indicate context, or the background of the Triple Self-Portrait can be empty of suggestion. Encourage the team to be as creative as they want to be, but to focus on the self-portrait nature of the task. Tell them that this is their chance to show their true selves. Be sure each "artist" signs his or her work.

When all are finished drawing, hang the pictures on a wall, gallery style, or spread them all out on several tables for viewing by the team.

Discussion Questions

Ask each artist to explain his or her drawing to the group after everyone has had a chance to view all pictures.

> Art has always been a way for people to express ideas and emotions through line, color, composition, and texture. Often in teamwork, you need a way to interrupt the flow of projects and deadlines to allow team members to express themselves differently. The fact that not everyone's an artist doesn't matter—it's the focus on three representations of self that makes this game fun and informative in a way unlike many others!

Materials

At least one sheet of drawing paper per team member; pencils, pens, markers, crayons, colored pencils, erasers; a copy of Norman Rockwell's *Triple Self-Portrait,* if possible.

Approximate Time Required

30–45 minutes.

Triple Self-Portrait

☐ **1.** a back view of the artist,

☐ **2.** a mirror reflecting the front view of the artist, and

☐ **3.** a canvas on which the finished portrait is emerging.

97

Behind the Scenes

Objective

To stretch the imagination by looking for visual patterns and imagining smells, sounds, tastes, and touch "behind" the obvious representation in a picture.

Procedure

Do this at a workshop or training session in which you want to encourage creative thinking by expanding the awareness and use of the five senses (sight, smell, hearing, taste, and touch).

Enlist the help of several team members prior to the workshop by asking them to bring in pictures from home to use in the workshop. Get four pictures of substantial size, at least 20×36-inch. The subject matter should be varied:

- one outdoor scene of water, trees, birds, or animals;

- one indoor scene with people and furnishings;

- one commercial scene with buildings, vehicles, machinery, and people;

- one festival scene such as Mardi Gras or a street-fair scene.

It doesn't matter who the artists were; what's important is that there is sufficient detail in the paintings to evoke the five senses.

Set up the paintings for all to see. Use small table-top easels or simply set the pictures up on chairs visible to all. Ask team members to "look behind the scenes" to see the paintings differently. Do this as an open response game, with team members calling out their responses as they think of them. Focus on the paintings one at a time.

Discussion Questions

First deal with the five senses, saving sight for last. Ask team members *if they were inside of the painting* what they would smell, hear, taste, or touch. Repeat the questions for each of the paintings. Encourage shy participants who

Notes

never thought about looking at a painting this way. Encourage more lively participants to imagine what scenes came before or after the one in the painting.

Then ask them to shift their thinking and get outside of the painting. Ask them to put themselves in the position of the artist who "designed" the painting. Now ask them what geometric patterns or color patterns they can see in each of the paintings, that is, what the design elements of each work of art were.

Teamwork requires expansive thinking—seeing things differently, seeing more than the obvious. This game creates awareness of this kind of thinking and gives team members some practice in thinking this way.

Materials

4 paintings brought from home; easels.

Approximate Time Required

30–45 minutes.

98
Fishtank

Objective

To experience thinking from a different perspective through a puzzle project.

Procedure

This is a team project to be done at two or more tables, depending on the size of your team. For it, you will need three jigsaw puzzles per table; that is, if you have the team divided around two tables, you'll need six puzzles altogether.

The object of the game is to force a paradigm shift in the learner/player's thinking processes regarding seeing the big picture and planning a project within it. To play this game, participants must work together as a team (subteam) at creating a fishtank from among the pieces of the 3 puzzles on the tables. The problem is that none of the puzzles is a fishtank puzzle, so that to play the game, participants have to figure out a way to use the pieces of the puzzle in a new way, thus the shift in thinking. The task at hand is to create a fishtank, not to solve the puzzles in the customary fashion.

Buy different kinds of puzzles, but none of fish or fishtanks. Some suggestions are: still life, children playing, animals, a carnival or circus, outdoor subjects like the seacoast or a forest scene.

You will be amazed at people's creativity: Some will build a three-dimensional fishtank, stacking pieces on top of each other; others will pick out similarly colored pieces from among all of the puzzles to put together the inhabitants of the fishtank; others will "draw" the outlines of the fishtank in two-dimensional perspective using puzzle pieces to make the outline. The possibilities are numerous in this different kind of puzzle. Don't necessarily tell team members what the possibilities are; they will figure out something to do on their own.

Start the game by simply saying that this is a game in experiencing a different way of thinking. Then announce

Notes

that the task for the next 20 minutes is to create a fishtank with the puzzles on the table. Set a timer and take stock of where everyone is at the 20-minute mark.

Discussion Questions

After the timer goes off, stop and ask team members to describe their way of thinking in creating the fishtank. Ask them to focus on whether they were leaders or followers in the task, what came into their heads at the beginning, how they negotiated with each other to decide what to do, etc. Suggest that team projects at work often require the same kinds of skills.

> There are many variations of this game. It's fun to design the game around the nature of your business, for example, a team of health care workers might build a hospital, instead of a fishtank; a team of clergy might build a church or a temple.

Materials

3 jigsaw puzzles of varying subjects per team table; a timer.

Approximate Time Required

20–30 minutes.

99

Interior Decorator

Objective

To rearrange a meeting room so that it is "better for teamwork."

Procedure

This is a team project, requiring leadership, followership, negotiation, goal setting, planning, and execution of plans. It is fun to do at a workshop, especially one held at a hotel where chairs and tables are movable and the room is a "generic" room, that is, not customized with company materials.

At the beginning of the session, after everyone has been seated, tell them that the first project of the day is to rearrange the furniture and redecorate the meeting place so that it is more team-friendly. Have available to them a table full of colored paper, colored markers, large paper such as newsprint from flip charts, uninflated balloons, paper streamers, plain white 8½×11-inch paper, blank name tags, colored yarn or string, tape, and scissors.

Tell team members that they have to think like interior decorators and assess the "feel" of the place and the "needs and wants" of the "owners." They can appoint a "head decorator" if they choose, and assume other roles appropriate for the task, or they can do the job as a consensus team. There's no right or wrong approach. Suggest that they consider all angles: furniture placement, space and closed areas, light, music, art on the walls, and ways for the "owners" to express their individual identity within the whole new environment. Suggest that the room will stay this way for the remainder of the team workshop, so it needs to be designed with the full day in mind.

Discussion Questions

After they have completed the task of redecoration, ask team members to describe the actions they took to work to-

Notes

gether to accomplish this assigned task. Ask them why they made the choices they made and why the room is now more team-friendly than it was when they came into it.

> This is an exercise in taking assertive action on behalf of teaming. Too often, companies new to the flatter structures of organizations fail to consider basic things like the environment for teamwork that may or may not exist in their workplaces. Team members have to be willing to speak up and make changes. This game will help fire them up to do just that.

Materials

A table full of creative paper construction materials; blank white paper of various sizes; tape, scissors, and markers of all sorts and colors.

Approximate Time Required

30–60 minutes.

100
Tell Me You Love Me

Objective

To signal team members to tell someone else that they appreciate what that person has accomplished.

Procedure

This game is akin to wearing a club or fraternity lapel pin to indicate brotherhood, sisterhood, and belonging. In this case, the symbol on the lapel is a cue to acknowledge someone else's accomplishment.

This game is best played for a specific time period, such as during a three-day conference or workshop, or for one week or one month on the job. At the start of the play period, give each team member a supply of blank self-stick name tags (4 to 6 name tags should be enough) to use to make the lapel markers. They are inexpensive, generally come in a package of 250, and are available at office supply stores. Patterns for the lapel markers are included on page 281. Each team member should make three of each letter, I, W, C, J, and A, as a supply of various messages to use over the time of play.

The idea of the game is to remind each other that a little appreciation goes a long way in the work of a team. People are not accustomed to complimenting each other in workplaces that reward individual excellence. To work together successfully in teams, however, that individual-is-king mind-set must be replaced by a mind-set that acknowledges the small, daily, even minute-by-minute accomplishments of each person on the team.

To play, ask each team member to choose a lapel marker according to the message he or she wants to send to teammates. Only one marker should be worn at a time. Markers can be changed as often as the wearer chooses to change them, or the same marker can remain for days. These are the choices:

Notes

I	=	Make me feel **I**mportant.
W	=	Tell me I'm **W**orth it.
C	=	Show me that you **C**are.
J	=	Say I did a good **J**ob.
A	=	**A**sk me; I'll tell you.

Discussion Questions

The lapel marker is the question. Each time a team member sees a fellow team member's lapel marker, he or she should respond to the message on the marker. Extend the game as long as anyone wants to keep going—months, if you're getting results! Post a cue card (or make a copy of page 281) somewhere in a central location so that all can check it in case they forget what each letter stands for.

It is said that Mary Kay, CEO of Mary Kay Cosmetics, has instituted a similar "game": Her version is that all employees have an invisible sign hanging around their necks that says, "Make Me Feel Important!" This version goes beyond that, but the intent is very much the same. Appreciation from fellow workers, especially team members, is a great motivator to do more good work.

Materials

Several sets of lapel markers per team member; plain self-stick name tags from which to cut the letters; pattern on page 281.

Approximate Time Required

Several hours, days, weeks, or months.

Tell Me You Love Me

I	=	Make me feel **I**mportant.
W	=	Tell me I'm **W**orth it.
C	=	Show me that you **C**are.
J	=	Say I did a good **J**ob.
A	=	**A**sk me; I'll tell you.

About the Author

Carolyn Nilson is a training consultant to many of the world's most successful, prestigious, and forward-looking corporations. These include: the ARINC Companies, AT&T, Chemical Bank, Chevron, Martin Marietta, Nabisco, and the World Bank. Dr. Nilson has also consulted with government agencies: the National Institute of Education, the U.S. Department of Education, the U.S. Department of Labor, and state departments of education. She has recently been a speaker at national conferences of the American Society for Training and Development (ASTD), the American Management Association, and the Center for the Study of Work Teams at the University of North Texas. She has been a faculty member at the American Management Associations's Padgett-Thompson Division Seminars, the Ziff Institute, and the U.S. Armed Services Training Institute. A former training executive, she held management positions in state-of-the art training applications at AT&T Bell Laboratories and at Combustion Engineering.

Dr. Nilson's work has been featured in recent editions of business magazines: *Successful Meetings, Training, Training & Development, Entrepreneur,* and *Fortune.* Her books have been chosen by MacMillan's Executive Program Book Club, the Newbridge Book Club, and Business Week Book Club. Her books have been reviewed by Lakewood Publications and ASTD, and featured in Lakewood's and ASTD's publications. She is the author of thirteen previous training books, among them the popular *Team Games for Trainers* and *Games That Drive Change,* published by McGraw-Hill. She is coauthor with Ed Scannell and John Newstrom of McGraw-Hill's new *Complete Games Trainers Play II.*